What is Sociology?

European Perspectives
A Series of the Columbia University Press

D1288049

What Is Sociology?

Norbert Elias

Translated by Stephen Mennell
and Grace Morrissey

With a Foreword by Reinhard Bendix

Columbia University Press
New York   1978

Translation published in 1978 in Great Britain by Hutchinson & Co.
(Publishers) Ltd and in the United States of America by Columbia
University Press

Library of Congress Cataloging in Publication Data

Elias, Norbert.
  What is sociology?

  (European perspectives)
  Translation of Was ist Soziologie?
  Includes bibliographical references and index.
  1. Sociology. I. Title.
HM57.E5813 1978   301   78–2386
ISBN 0–231–04550–6

Printed in Great Britain

Contents

Author's acknowledgements

If, in writing an introduction to sociology, one deviates somewhat from the familiar paths and in doing so endeavours to help the reader to think through anew the basic problems of society, in the first instance one can trust to nothing else but one's own conscience. Yet one is always dependent on other people for their help, encouragement, stimulus, and suggestions. Here I cannot name everyone who in one way or another has aided me in this work. But apart from the Editor of the series, Professor Dieter Claessens, to whom I dedicate this book, I must explicitly mention Dr W. Lepenies, who with great skill and tact adjusted the author's over-long, rather difficult and not easily shortened manuscript to the prescribed format for the series. Volker Krumrey gave me indispensable help and good advice on the preparation of the manuscript. I should also like to express my heartfelt thanks to my friends and colleagues Eric Dunning, Johan Goudsblom and Hermann Korte for the stimulus and advice they gave me. Finally, I must not omit to thank my publisher Dr M. Faltermaier, whose patience I from time to time sorely tried.

Norbert Elias
Leicester, 1969

Translators' acknowledgements

The principal debt which Grace Morrissey and I owe as translators of *What is Sociology?* is to the author himself. One of the chief purposes of Professor Elias's book is to invite sociologists to re-structure their imaginations, to *re*consider the way they think and speak about society. And so, in many instances, our knowledge of current sociological idiom proved something of a handicap – the problem was precisely to avoid the familiar terms and modes of expression. In this, the author's assistance has been more than valuable; it has been essential. As a sociologist rather than as trans-lator, I should like to acknowledge the stimulus I gained through my conversations with Professor Elias.

In revising the translation for publication I was immensely assisted by Professor Johan Goudsblom of the University of Amsterdam, who read the entire text and constructively criticized it line by line. Rod Aya, Donald Munro, Gillian Middleton-Smith, my wife Barbara and, indirectly, my fellow contributors to the *Festschrift* for Norbert Elias (*Human Figurations*, edited by Gleichmann Goudsblom and Korte, Amsterdam 1977) also suggested many improvements. Beryl Harris, Elsa Broome and Sue Ridler typed the manuscript.

Lastly, let me thank Ann Douglas and her successor at Hutchinson, Robert Shreeve, who encouraged me to persist with this translation; their patience, like that of the original German publisher, was sorely tried.

Stephen Mennell
Exeter, 1977

Foreword

Norbert Elias is one of the German scholars who fled Germany in the 1930s and eventually made his home in England. His most important scholarly contribution, *Über den Prozess der Zivilisation,* was published in 1939 in Switzerland, and a new edition with an important new introduction was published in 1969, also in Switzerland. It is only now, however, that Elias's major works, including the present volume, are becoming available to English readers. Nevertheless, Norbert Elias's work as a teacher at the University of Leicester had considerable influence. By now one can speak of a whole generation of English sociologists who have been students of Elias and carried away with them his infectious enthusiasm for the subject. Readers of this book will be able to recognize what has captured their imagination, the author's natural gift as a teacher. It is also possible to speak of a renewed interest in the work of Elias in Germany and Holland where, after his retirement from Leicester in 1962, he has been visiting professor at several universities. In effect, Norbert Elias's fate has been singular in that his major impact as a teacher has been in England, while the belated impact of his scholarly work has remained within the German academic world.

What is Sociology? was published originally in 1970, a late product of the author's career. In the very last sentence of its last note he says: 'every later theory develops both as a continuation of earlier theories and yet as a critical departure from them'. Though this statement refers to Marx, it applies equally well to Elias. The reader finds in this deceptively slight introduction a new vindication of sociology by recourse to basic ideas first outlined by Auguste Comte. Further, Elias restates basic categories of sociological thought and thus continues the 'sociological tradition' while taking a critical stance towards major contributors such as Marx, Weber, and Parsons. In the process he induces the reader to think with him about such fundamental terms of sociological discourse as *society, individual, group,* and others.

The inspiration for this approach derives from the author's own socio-historical work, which deals with changing patterns of inter-dependence in relation to the power-relations among men in society. The earlier analysis of changing norms of etiquette in relation to the emergence of monarchical 'absolutism' (in medieval France) was followed by a later study of Court Society (*Die höfische Gesellschaft,* 1969). In both works the author emphasizes that out of

the interweaving of innumerable individual interests and intentions – be they compatible, or opposed and inimical – something eventually emerges that, as it turns out, has neither been planned nor intended by any single individual. And yet it has been brought about by the intentions and actions of many individuals. And this is actually the whole secret of social interweaving – of its compellingness, its regularity, its structure, its processual nature, and its development; this is the secret of socio-genesis and social dynamics. [*Über den Prozess der Zivilisation* (1969), II, p. 221.]

Of course, Elias makes clear that in these interdependencies rulers like kings, high officials, and others have influence of broader scope, but he also insists that they themselves remain part of the inter-dependencies in which they are relatively dominant (*Die höfische Gesellschaft* (Neuwied: Hermann Luchterhand Verlag, 1969), pp. 213–21).

By systematically relating this approach to history and to differ-entials of power, Norbert Elias has made a major contribution to modern sociology. The present introduction can be read with profit in its own terms, but the reader should be aware that *What is Sociology?* is based on scholarly work that combines political history, depth psychology, and sociology in a unique synthesis of considerable power.

˘ Reinhard Bendix
University of California, Berkeley

Introduction

To understand what sociology is all about, one has to look at oneself from a distance, to see oneself as one human being among others. For sociology is concerned with problems of society, and society is something formed by oneself and other people together; the person who studies and thinks about society is himself a member of it. Thinking about oneself in contemporary society, it is often difficult to escape the feeling that one is facing other human beings just as if they were mere objects, separated from oneself by an unbridgeable gulf. This sense of separation is expressed, reproduced and reinforced through many current concepts and idioms, which make this modern mode of self-experience appear self-evident and incontestable. We speak of the individual and his environment, of the child and his family, of individual and society, or of subject and object, without clearly reminding ourselves that the individual forms part of his environment, his family, his society. Looking more closely, the so-called 'environment' of the child consists primarily of other human beings, of father, mother, brothers and sisters. What we conceptualize as 'family' would not be a family at all without children. Society, often placed in mental contraposition to the individual, consists entirely of individuals, oneself among them.

Yet our conventional instruments for thinking and speaking are generally constructed as though everything we experience as external to the individual were a thing, an 'object', and more-over a stationary object. Concepts like 'family' or 'school' plainly refer to groupings of interdependent human beings, to specific figurations which people form with each other. But our traditional manner of forming these concepts makes it appear as if groupings formed by interdependent human beings were pieces of matter – objects of the same kind as rocks, trees or houses. These traditional reifying ways of speaking, and corresponding tradi-

tional modes of thinking about groupings of people – even groupings to which one belongs oneself – manifest themselves in many
ways, not least in the term 'society' and the way one handles it
in one's thinking. It is customary to say that society is the
'thing' which sociologists investigate. But this reifying mode of
expression greatly hampers and may even prevent one from
understanding the nature of sociological problems.

The commonsense model which today dominates people's
experience of their own, or any other individual's, relationship
to society is naïvely egocentric, as indicated in Figure 1. Figura-

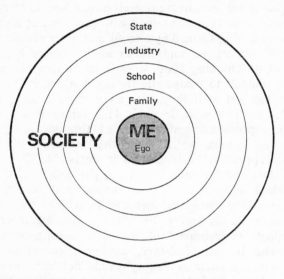

Fig 1   *Basic pattern of the egocentric view of society*

tions like university, town, system and countless others can be
substituted for family, school, industry or state. Whatever they
are, the predominant and typical way of conceptualizing such
social groupings, and the mode of self-perception it expresses,
generally corresponds to the diagram above, which shows the
individual person, the particular ego, surrounded by social structures. These are understood to be objects over and above the
individual ego. The concept of 'society' is also seen in this way.

To understand better the problematics of sociology, or what is
usually referred to as its 'subject-matter', one needs to reorientate one's comprehension of the concept 'society', in the way

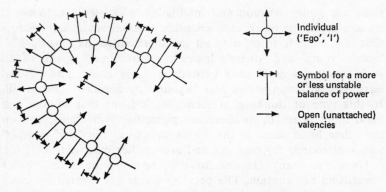

Individual
('Ego', 'I')

Symbol for a more
or less unstable
balance of power

Open (unattached)
valencies

Fig 2 *A figuration of interdependent individuals ('family', 'state', 'group', 'society', etc.)*[1*]

implied by Figure 2. This diagram should help the reader to break through the brittle façade of reifying concepts which obscure and distort our understanding of our own life in society. Time and time again they encourage the impression that society is made up of structures external to oneself, the individual, and that the individual is at one and the same time surrounded by society yet cut off from it by some invisible barrier. As we shall see, these traditional ideas have to be replaced by a different, more realistic picture of people who, through their basic dispositions and inclinations, are directed towards and linked with each other in the most diverse ways. These people make up webs of interdependence or figurations of many kinds, characterized by power balances of many sorts, such as families, schools, towns, social strata, or states. Every one of these people is, as it is often put in a reifying manner, an ego or self. Among these people belongs also oneself.

To understand what sociology is all about one must, as we have said, be aware of oneself as a human being among other human beings. At first hearing, that sounds like a cliché. Villages and towns, universities and factories, estates and classes, families and occupational groups – all these are networks of individuals. Each one of us belongs among these individuals – that is what we express in saying '*my* village, *my* university, *my* class, *my* country'. At the level of everyday usage, such expres-

*Superior figures refer to *Notes and references* on pages 175-82.

sions are quite common and intelligible. Nevertheless, today, if we are trying to think in a scientific manner we usually forget that it is possible to refer to all social structures as 'mine', 'his', 'ours', 'yours' and 'theirs'. Instead, we habitually speak of all such structures as if they existed not only above and beyond ourselves but even above and beyond any actual people at all. In this type of thinking, it seems self-evident that on the one hand there is an 'I', or there are particular individuals, and on the other hand there is the social structure, the 'environment' which surrounds my own self and every other particular I.

There are many reasons for this; here we need only point towards an explanation. The peculiar constraint exerted by social structures over those who form them is particularly significant. We tend to explain away this compulsion by ascribing to these structures an existence – an objective reality – over and above the individuals who make them up. The prevailing ways of forming words and concepts further enhance the tendency in our thinking to reify and dehumanize social structures. This in turn leads to the characteristic 'metaphysic of social structures', now encountered as often in everyday thinking as in sociological thought. One of its most typical expressions is in the image of the relationship between individual and society symbolized in Figure 1.

This metaphysic is further sustained by the automatic displacement of ways of thinking and speaking first developed and tested in the investigation of natural relationships in physics and chemistry, into the investigation of social relationships between individuals. Before a scientific approach to natural events became possible, people explained the natural forces to which they felt subject in terms of modes of thinking and speaking that had arisen out of their experience of interpersonal forces. The sun and earth, or storms and earthquakes, which nowadays we understand as manifestations of natural physico-chemical forces, they interpreted in terms of their own immediate experience of human and social phenomena. They saw them either as persons or as the results of the actions and designs of persons. Only gradually did the transition come about from magical and metaphysical thinking to scientific thinking about the physico-chemical aspects of the world. The change was to a large degree dependent on the fading away of heteronomous, naïvely egocentric explanatory models, the functions of which were assumed by other models

of speech and thought corresponding more closely to the immanent dynamics of natural events.

In trying to enlarge our understanding of human and social
processes and to acquire a growing fund of more reliable knowledge about them – this in itself is one of the main objects of
sociology – we are confronted with a similar task of emancipation. In this sphere, too, people find themselves subjected to
'compelling forces'. They seek to understand them so that with
the help of this knowledge they may gain some control over the
blind course of these compelling forces, the effects of which for
them are often senseless and destructive, causing much suffering.
The aim is to guide these forces in such a way as to make them
less meaningless and less wasteful of lives and resources. It is
therefore central to the tasks of sociological teaching and
research to acquire a general understanding of these forces and
an increase in dependable knowledge about them through
specialized fields of investigation.

The first step does not seem very difficult. It is not hard to
grasp the idea that what we attempt to conceptualize as social
forces are in fact forces exerted by people over one another and
over themselves. Yet as soon as we try to proceed from here, we
find that the social apparatus for thinking and speaking places at
our disposal only either models of a naïvely egocentric or magico-
mythical kind, or else models from natural science. We encounter
the former whenever people try to explain the compelling forces
stemming from the figurations they and other people form
together, entirely in terms of the personal character or the personal aims and intentions of *other* individuals or groups of
individuals. This urge to except oneself or one's own group from
explanation in terms of figurations formed with other people is
very common, and it is one of the many manifestations of naïve
egocentricity or (what is much the same) naïve anthropomorphism
which still permeate our thought and speech about social processes. These naïvely egocentric modes of expression are mixed
with others which, modelled on the vocabulary used to explain
compelling forces of nature, are now used to explain the compelling forces found in society.

There has been a trend towards 'scientificization' of modes of
speaking and thinking about what is now known to be inanimate
nature, in sharp distinction from the human-social world. Many
verbal and conceptual structures derived from the uncovering of

physical and chemical structures have passed into the everyday stock of words and concepts of European society and taken root there. Numerous words and concepts, the present-day forms of which derive primarily from the interpretation of natural events, have been transferred unobtrusively to the interpretation of human and social phenomena. Together with the various manifestations of magico-mythical thought, they contribute to the perpetuation of many customary modes of speech and thought for tackling problems in the human sciences to which they are plainly unsuited. They thus hinder the development of more autonomous ways of speaking and thinking, better suited to the special peculiarities of human figurations.

The tasks of sociology therefore include not only examination and interpretation of specific compelling forces to which people are exposed in their particular empirically observable societies and groups, but also the freeing of speech and thought about such forces from their links with earlier heteronomous models. In place of words and concepts bearing the mark of their origin in magico-mythical ideas or in natural science, sociology must gradually develop others which do better justice to the peculiarities of human social figurations.

This would be less difficult if today we already had a clear picture of the corresponding phase in the development of the natural sciences, when new and more adequate means of speaking and thinking replaced the older magico-mythical ones. Of this, however, we know very little. Many of the gradually developed fundamental concepts of the scientific knowledge of nature proved again and again to be more or less appropriate in the observation and manipulation of physico-chemical processes. For this very reason, these fundamental concepts appear to their inheritors to be eternally valid and, therefore, eternal. The corresponding scientific words, categories and modes of thought seem so self-evident that it is easy to imagine that every human being knew them intuitively. It took numerous generations of scientists much hard thought and observation, arduous and often very dangerous struggles to develop ideas like those of mechanical causality or the non-intentional, aimless and unplanned lawfulness of nature. Only very slowly and with great difficulty did these ideas emerge out of anthropomorphic and egocentric ideas and ways of thinking. Then finally the new ideas diffused outwards from a small élite, until they informed the everyday thought and speech of

whole social groups. Now they often appear to subsequent generations to be simply 'true', 'rational' or 'logical' ideas and modes of
thought. By and large they stand the test of constant observation
and action, and we therefore no longer ask how and why human
thinking about this particular level of integration in the cosmos
has become so well adapted to its purpose.

Therefore, it emerges that these social developments of speech
and thought about the compelling forces of natural processes have
been neglected as a subject for sociological research. The static
philosophical idea of scientific knowledge as an 'eternally human'
form of knowledge has almost completely inhibited inquiry into
the sociogenesis and psychogenesis of the scientific vocabulary
and modes of speech and thought. Yet only investigations such as
these will put us on the right track in explaining this reorientation
of human thought and experience. The problem is usually discounted before it is posed, because it is seen as 'merely an
historical matter', as opposed to so-called problems of systematic
theory. But this distinction is itself an illustration of the inadequacy of natural scientific models for comprehending long-
term social processes, of which the scientificization of thought is
one. Such processes are quite different from what is called the
history of science, as contrasted with an apparently immutable
philosophy of science, just as natural history used to be contrasted
with the study of the apparently immutable solar system.

Corresponding to this failure to investigate problems of long-
term processes of social development, we still lack a general
understanding of the long-term reorientation of language and
thought in European societies, to which the rise of the natural
sciences would be central. Such an understanding is essential if we
are to gain a clearer and more vivid picture of the transformation.
It would also make it much easier for people to understand that
sociology has now reached a new level of experience and awareness. With constant feedback from the increasing volume of
empirical research we can now discard many traditional models
of knowledge and thought, and over the years develop in their
place other instruments for speaking and thinking, better suited
to the scientific investigation of human social figurations.

Emancipation from heteronomous ideas, with their concomitant
modes of speech and thought, is scarcely easier for the human
sciences than it was for the natural sciences two or three centuries
ago. Those espousing the cause of the natural sciences then had

no choice but to start by combating institutionalized magico-mythical models of perception and thought; protagonists of the social sciences today must now also struggle against the heteronomous use of natural scientific models which have become just as firmly institutionalized.

Even bearing in mind that social forces are forces exerted by people over themselves and over one another, it is still very difficult when thinking and speaking to guard against the social pressure of verbal and conceptual structures. These make social forces seem like forces exerted on objects in nature – like forces external to people, exerted over them as 'objects'. Too often we speak and think as though not just mountains, clouds and storms, but also villages and states, the economy and politics, factors of production and technological advances, the sciences and the industrial system, among countless other social structures, were all extra-human entities with their own inner laws and thus quite independent of human action or inaction. They appear, in the sense of Figure 1, to be 'society' or 'the environment', exerting influence over every human being, every single 'I'. Many of the nouns that are used in the social sciences – and in everyday speech – are formed and used as if they referred to material things, visible and tangible objects in time and space, existing independently of people.

However, that is not to say that we could already manage the business of teaching and research without this kind of word and concept structure. No matter how painfully aware we are of their inadequacy, more adequate means of thought and communication are in many instances simply not available at present. We might consistently try to free the current stock of language and knowledge, now used to extend our understanding of human networks and social figurations, from heteronomous models of speech and thought. We might try to substitute more autonomous models for them. Yet any such attempt would at present be doomed to failure. Certain social transformations can only be achieved, if at all, by long and sustained development spanning several generations. This reorientation of speech and thought is one of them. It requires much linguistic and conceptual innovation. Rushing it would jeopardize its chances of being understood at the present time. Of course, in favourable circumstances single neologisms can pass into social usage very quickly. But affinity and understanding for new ways of speaking and thinking never develop without conflict with older and more familiar ones. What is necessary is a reorganization of perception and thought on the part of all the many interdependent people in a society. If a great many people are to relearn and rethink all this and to accustom themselves to a whole complex of new concepts – or old concepts with new meanings – then a time-span of two or three generations is usually needed, sometimes much longer. For all that, a clearer view of the common task in hand may perhaps facilitate and speed up a reorientation even of such a magnitude. My purpose here is to contribute to this clarification.

With this purpose in mind, a discussion of the difficulty and slowness of such a reorientation of social language and thought may itself give an impression of the kind of forces which people exert over each other. It would be less difficult to understand that such forces are quite distinctive, if our language and thought were not so thoroughly permeated with words and concepts like 'casual necessity', 'determinism', 'scientific law' and others of the same sort. These denote models derived from practical experience in the realm of natural science, of physics and chemistry. Later they have been transferred to other areas of experience, for which they were not originally intended at all, among them the realm of human relationships which we call society. In the process, awareness of their original connections with discoveries about physico-chemical sequences of events has been lost. So now they seem to be quite general concepts, even to some extent *a priori* conceptions of how events are connected; all men seem to possess them as part of their innate 'commonsense' or 'reason', independent of experience.

In most cases, when entering a new area of experience, one is simply faced with a lack of concepts appropriate to the types of forces and relationships encountered there. Take for example the notion of 'force'. Our use of a common language to communicate with each other exerts a kind of force over the speech and thought of individual people. This kind of force is of a quite different type from, for example, the force of gravity which, in accordance with scientific laws, pulls a ball back to earth when it is thrown high in the air. Yet what distinctive and special concepts are available today which can express this difference clearly and intelligibly? Scientific societies perhaps have greater scope for making linguistic and intellectual innovations than do other types of society. Even so, their scope is not unlimited. If it is stretched too far, there is a risk of failing to be understood by other people. Furthermore, one's own speech and thought is normally controlled by others, and if this control is broken entirely, one also runs the risk of losing control over oneself, or losing oneself in limitless speculation, in fantasies, and playing around with ideas. It is very difficult to steer a course between the Scylla of physics and the Charybdis of metaphysics.

Too much should not be expected from a single book. Such a truly radical reorientation and renewal as is now beginning, heralded by efforts to define social relationships sociologically, cannot be sustained throughout by the imaginative and inventive powers of any one individual. It needs the convergent efforts of many people. In the end, the critical factor is the direction of overall social development – the development of the human network as a whole. A strong wave of new ideas may influence the course of overall social development, provided that fluctuating trends in the distribution of power and consequent struggles for power do not bring reorientation to a complete standstill and destroy the impulse behind it. In their present situation, the social sciences encounter the same difficulty which afflicted the natural sciences during the centuries of their rise: that the greater the anger and passion aroused by the conflict, the less the chance of a changeover to more realistic, less fantasy-laden thinking. And the more fantasy-laden – the further from reality – their thinking, the more uncontrollable are people's anger and passion. In antiquity, a conception of nature more in keeping with reality arose briefly; but it was subsequently destroyed by the onset of a new bout of mythologizing connected with the absorption of smaller, self-governing states by great imperial states. This shows how fragile and precarious a premature attempt at change can be. Another example is the development of utopian ideas out of scientific social thought during the nineteenth and twentieth centuries. Both examples point to a vicious circle which is itself one of the compelling forces in need of more precise investigation. Some reference to it may shed a little light on the trend towards scientificization of thought, which has not as yet received the attention it deserves.[2]

One characteristic which distinguishes the scientific from the prescientific way of acquiring knowledge is that the scientific is more closely connected with the real world of objects. The scientific way gives people a chance to distinguish more clearly, as they proceed, between fanciful and realistic ideas. At first hearing, that may sound over-simplified. The strong current of philosophical nominalism, which still swamps and obscures epistemological thought, has brought concepts like 'reality' and 'fact' into disrepute. But the question here is not one of philosophical speculation, whether of a nominalist or a positivist kind, but of establishing something about the theory of science that can be verified by detailed observations, and if necessary revised. At one time, people imagined that the moon was a goddess. Today we have a more adequate, more realistic idea of the moon. Tomorrow it may be discovered that there are still elements of fantasy in our present idea of the moon, and people may develop a conception of the moon, the solar system and the whole universe still closer to reality than ours. The comparative which qualifies this assertion is important; it can be used to steer ideas between the two towering, unmoving philosophical cliffs of nominalism and positivism, to keep in the current of the long-term development of knowledge and thought. We are describing the direction of this current in calling special attention to the decrease in the fanciful elements and increase in the realistic elements in our thinking, as characteristics of the scientificization of our ways of thinking and acquiring knowledge. To investigate changes in the balance, the relative frequency and weight of elements of fantasy and of realism in our accepted ideas about human societies would require far closer study than is possible here. Both concepts are many-layered. That of fantasy, for example, can refer to individual dreams, to day-dreams and wish-fulfilment, to imaginative expression through art, to metaphysical speculation, to collective belief-systems or ideologies, and much else besides.

One kind of fantasy, however, played a quite indispensable role in the process of scientificization and the process by which people gained increasing mastery over reality. That was the kind of fantasy which was both kept in check and made fruitful by close contact with factual observation. Nominalist philosophers as a rule disdain to draw the complex relation of fact and fantasy into their meditations and to assimilate it conceptually. Consequently they are hardly in a position to explain to their audience the effects of the increasing scientificization of thinking about non-human natural phenomena. As this process continues, with constant feedback on to practical affairs, it may increase people's chances of avoiding danger from natural events, and their chances of turning towards goals of their own choosing. For example, how can the improvement in standards of living and health in many societies be explained, except by our knowledge and thinking about these fields having become less emotionally-charged and fantasy-laden, less magico-mythical and more objective and realistic?

Nowadays many people, including sociologists, talk about the sciences with noticeable discomfort, sometimes even with a certain contempt. 'What have all these scientific discoveries – machines, factories, cities, nuclear bombs and all the other horrors of scientific warfare – done for us?' they ask. This argument is a typical example of the suppression of an unwelcome explanation and the substitution of a more welcome one (a process called 'displacement'). The hydrogen bomb was after all developed at the instigation of statesmen, who would be the ones to order its use if they thought it necessary. Yet to us the nuclear bomb serves as a kind of fetish, an object onto which we project our fears, while the real danger lies in the reciprocal hostility displayed by groups of people in their relations with each other. To some extent even their hostility makes the hostile groups dependent on each other, and they can become so deeply enmeshed in it that they can no longer see any way out of the situation. We blame the bomb, and the scientists whose reality-orientated research made it possible, as a pretext for concealing from ourselves our complicity in the reciprocal hostility, or at least our individual helplessness in the face of the apparent inevitability of threat and counter-threat. By blaming the scientists, we also evade our obligation to seek a more realistic explanation of the social entanglements which lead to a gradually escalating exchange of threats between groups of people. The complaint that we have become 'slaves of the machine' or of technology is similar. Despite science-fiction nightmares, machines have no will of their own. They can neither invent nor produce themselves, and cannot compel us to serve them. All decisions and activities they carry out are human decisions and activities. We project threats and compulsions on to them, but if we look more closely we always see interdependent groups of people threatening and compelling each other by means of machines. When people blame their uneasiness about life in scientific-technical-industrial societies on to bombs or machines, scientists or engineers, they are evading the difficult and maybe unpleasant task of seeking a clearer, more realistic interpretation of the structure of human interweavings and particularly of the patterns of conflict rooted in them. It is this structure which is responsible for the development and eventual use of scientific weapons of war, and for the hardships of life in factories and modern metropolises. Technological developments do indeed influence the direction in which human interweavings develop. But the technical 'thing in itself' is never the source of the compelling forces and hardship to which people are subject; these are always caused by the way people apply technology and fit it into the social framework. What we need to fear is not the destructive power of the nuclear bomb but that of human beings, or more accurately of human interweavings. The danger lies not in the progress of science and technology, but in the manner in which research findings and technological inventions are used by people under the pressure of their entangled interdependence, and in the associated struggles over the distribution of power chances of all kinds. In the following pages of this introduction to sociology, little will be said about these acute problems. The foremost concern of this book is to promote the development of sociological imagination and thinking towards a perception of these interweavings and figurations which people form. But a reminder about the acute problems which afflict social interweavings may be useful as an introduction.

The mental fixation on familiar and tangible phenomena like nuclear bombs and machines or, in a broader sense, on science and technology, obscuring the social causes of fear and unease, is symptomatic of one of the fundamental characteristics of our age. That is the discrepancy between, on the one hand, our relatively great ability nowadays to overcome – appropriately and realistically – problems caused by extra-human natural events, and, on the other hand, our comparatively limited ability to solve problems of human coexistence with anything approaching the same reliability.

In an odd way, we have double standards for thought, for perception, for the acquisition of knowledge and for knowledge itself. In the field of natural phenomena, all these processes are highly and increasingly realistic. This field may be infinite. But within it, the fund of relatively reliable, more realistic scientific knowledge grows continuously and cumulatively. The standard of self-discipline is relatively high, and personal egocentric views are counteracted by a relatively effective mutual control on the part of all investigators, directing their observations and thought primarily to the objects of investigation. There is relatively little latitude for egocentric or ethnocentric fantasies to influence the results of research, as they are held in check by careful comparison at each phase of a piece of research, and discounted. The high degree of self-control in consideration of natural phenomena, and the corresponding degree of object-centredness, realism and 'rationality' of thought and action in these fields, is no longer the monopoly of specialist researchers. They are now basic attitudes held by people in all the more developed industrial societies. In so far as our whole lives, even their most private aspects, have been technologized, these principles govern all our thoughts and actions. However, in our private lives there is still room for egocentric fantasies about natural phenomena, but people are quite often aware of them as just that – as personal fantasies.

In contrast, in the same societies there is still immense scope for egocentric and ethnocentric fantasies to constitute decisive factors in perception, thought and action in areas of social life unrelated to scientific and technological problems. In the social sciences, not even researchers have at their disposal common standards for mutual control and self-control which would allow them to scrutinize their colleagues' work as confidently as can their counterparts in the natural sciences. Nor is it so easy for them to distinguish between arbitrary personal fantasies or political and nationalistic ideals on the one hand, and reality-orientated theoretical models verifiable by empirical investigation on the other. And in society at large, social standards of thought about social problems still permit people to some extent to surrender to their own fantasies, without recognizing them as such. This recalls the extent of fantasies about natural events in the Middle Ages. In medieval times strangers, particularly Jews, were held responsible for outbreaks of the plague, and large groups of them were massacred. At that time people knew of no more realistic, scientific explanations to account for events like mass deaths in epidemics. As so often happens, the ruling groups poured their anxiety, as yet unchecked by more realistic knowledge, their fear of the inexplicable horrors of the plague, and their passionate anger at what they perceived as an incomprehensible attack, into fantasies in which they saw outsiders and socially weaker groups as the source of their own sufferings. The result was mass murder. During the nineteenth century, European societies were attacked by several waves of cholera epidemics. Thanks to the increase in state supervision of public health matters, and to the progress of scientific knowledge and the diffusion of scientific explanations of epidemics, this kind of large-scale infectious disease was finally brought under control. In the twentieth century, both the adequacy of science and the level of social prosperity have increased and made it possible to turn theories of public hygiene into practice by preventive measures. So for the first time since population densities began to increase, people living in Europe are at last almost entirely free from the threat of epidemic disease, and have almost forgotten about it. Yet our thoughts and actions with regard to human social coexistence are still at the same stage of development as medieval thought and behaviour with regard to the plague. In social matters, people are exposed even today to pressures and anxieties they cannot comprehend. Since people in distress are unable to live without some explanation, the gaps in understanding are filled out by fantasy.

In our time, the National Socialist myth was an example of this kind of interpretation of social distress and unrest, from which it sought relief through action. Here too, just as in the case of the plague, anxiety and unrest about social miseries found release in fantasy-laden explanations identifying socially weak minorities as the troublemakers and culprits, so leading to their slaughter. Thus we can see how it is characteristic of our times that a highly factual realistic grasp of physical and technical matters should exist alongside fantasy-laden solutions to social problems, which as yet we are either unwilling or unable to explain and overcome more adequately.

The National Socialist hope of solving social problems by exterminating the Jews seems a rather extreme example of what is in fact a universally prevalent feature of the present-day social life of mankind. Nevertheless, it demonstrates the function of fantasy-riddled explanations of social distress and anxiety, the real explanations of which we cannot or will not perceive. At the same time, it is symptomatic of a significant dualism in contemporary thought that a cloak of natural scientific, biological respectability should have to be draped round a social fantasy.

The word 'fantasy' sounds harmless enough. That fantasies play an indispensable, highly constructive role in human life is not disputed here. Like the ability to present many different facial expressions, to smile or to weep, the highly developed capacity for fantasy is a uniquely human characteristic. But here we refer to fantasy of a particular type, or more accurately to fantasies which are wrongly applied to social life. When not controlled by factual knowledge, this type of fantasy is, especially in a situation of crisis, among the most unreliable, often most murderous impulses governing human action. In such situations, people need not be insane for these impulses to be let loose.

Nowadays, we often like to think that the element of fantasy, which plays an important part in directing a group's common actions and ideas towards its goals, is merely a blind – nothing more than an alluring, exciting mask of propaganda. We imagine that cunning leaders use it to conceal their boldly-conceived aims which in terms of their 'own interests' are highly 'rational' or 'realistic'. Of course, that does sometimes happen. But when we use the concept of 'reason' in expressions like 'reasons of state', the concept of 'realism' in terms like *'Realpolitik'*, and many other similar concepts, we help to reinforce the widespread idea that rational, objective or realistic considerations are usually the main ones when groups of people quarrel. The use to which the concept of ideology is put – even by sociologists – shows the same tendency. But, on closer investigation, it is not very difficult to see the great extent to which both realistic and fantasy-laden ideas pervade the conception of 'group interests'. Realistic, methodical plans for social change – even makeshift ones – drawn up with the help of scientific models of development, are an innovation of very recent origin. Often the developmental models themselves are plainly still very imperfect, and do not yet correspond closely enough to the changing social structures to which they refer. The whole of history has so far amounted to no more than a grave-yard of human dreams. Dreams often find short-term fulfilment; but in the long run, they virtually always seem to end up drained of substance and meaning and so destroyed. The reason is that aims and hopes are so heavily saturated with fantasy that the actual course of events in society deals them blow after blow, and the shock of reality reveals them as unreal, in fact as dreams. The peculiar sterility of many analyses of ideologies largely stems from the tendency to treat them as basically rational structures of ideas coinciding with actual group interests. Their burden of affect and fantasy, their egocentric or ethnocentric lack of reality are overlooked, for they are assumed to be merely a calculated camouflage for a highly rational core.

As an example, consider the situation of conflict between the Great Powers which has persisted since the Second World War and which increasingly influences and overshadows conflicts within other states all over the world. The representatives of each of the Great Powers seem to imagine that they possess a unique national charisma and that they and their ideals alone are fitted for world leadership. It is very difficult to discover any realistic conflicts of interest which would account for the enormous escalation in preparations for war. The practical social differences between them are obviously much smaller than would be expected, bearing in mind the sharp contrasts between their belief systems and ideals. More than any conflict of interests that could be called 'real', it is a collision between the dreams of the Great Powers – and not only the great ones – which makes them so harshly and unremittingly hostile to each other. This now almost world-wide polarization has a considerable structural resemblance to an earlier European polarization when the dreams of Protestant and Catholic princes and generals came into collision. In those days, people were as passionately eager to kill each other wholesale for the sake of their belief systems as they now seem willing to kill wholesale for the reason that some prefer the Russian belief system, some the American or the Chinese. As far as one can see, it is mainly the contradiction between the belief systems of national states and their charismatic sense of national mission which renders this kind of interweaving opaque and incomprehensible to those caught up in them, and which therefore makes them uncontrollable. (The national belief systems, incidentally, have little to do with Marx's analysis of class antagonisms within states, an analysis that at his time was highly appropriate.)

This too is an example of the dynamics of social interweavings, the systematic investigation of which is the concern of sociology. At this level, the figurations are composed of interdependent groups of people, organized into national states, and not of single interdependent individuals. But here, too, the units to which people refer in the first person – not only the singular 'I' but also the plural 'we' – are experienced by them as if they were completely autonomous. As schoolchildren they were already learning that their own national state possessed unlimited 'sovereignty', that it was completely independent of all other states. The ethnocentric image of humanity divided into national states is analogous with the egocentric image expressed in Figure 1. The ruling élites and many of their followers in each nation (or at least in each Great Power) imagine themselves to be in the centre of humanity as if in a fortress, contained and surrounded by all the other nations, yet at the same time cut off from them. In this case too, the stage of self-awareness in thought and action expressed in Figure 2, but with nations as the basic units instead of single people, is scarcely ever reached.

At present, the conception of one's own nation as one among many other interdependent ones, and an understanding of the structure of the figurations they all form, has hardly begun to develop. It is rare to come across a clear sociological model of the dynamics of relationships between states. Take for example the dynamics of the 'cold war' between the Great Powers. Both sides involved in it seek to increase their own power potential out of fear of the power potential of their opponent. Thus their fears of each other are vindicated and they drive themselves on to increase their own power potential even further, which in turn spurs their opponent on to make a corresponding effort. Since no arbiter commands sufficient power chances to break this deadlock, unless both sides *simultaneously* gain an insight into the immanent dynamics of the figuration they form together, its compelling forces make further efforts to increase power potentials quite inevitable. But the interdependent opponents, and especially the party oligarchs on every side, do not attain this insight. Rather their dominant belief is that their own danger and constant efforts to increase their power potential can be fully explained by pointing to the other side, the opponents of the moment, with their 'wrong social system' and 'dangerous national beliefs'. Nations are as yet unable to see themselves as integral components of a figuration, the dynamics of which are compelling them to make these efforts. The rigidity of the polarized national belief system prevents the ruling party oligarchs from seeing sufficiently clearly that they themselves, their party traditions and the social ideals by which they justify their claims to rule, are constantly losing credibility. This credibility gap is caused by their actually helping to bring about dangerous confrontation in war, by their wasting on war materials the resources created by human labour, and ultimately by their actual use of force. Here again, this time in paradigmatic form, we find a highly realistic mastery of the physico-technological environment existing side by side with an extremely fantasy-laden approach to interpersonal, social, problems.

Looking around, it is not hard to find still further examples of this discrepancy. Nevertheless, many people today believe that it is possible to approach social problems from the standpoint of their own inborn 'rationality', quite independent of the current state of development of social knowledge and thought, yet with the same 'objective' approach that a physicist or engineer brings to scientific or technological problems.

Thus contemporary governments commonly assert – perhaps in good faith – that they can overcome the acute social problems of their country 'rationally' or 'realistically'. In fact, however, they usually fill the gaps in our still fairly rudimentary factual knowledge of the dynamics of social interweavings with dogmatic doctrines, handed-down nostrums, or considerations of short-term party interests. Taking measures mostly by chance, they remain at the mercy of events, the sequence of which governments understand as little as those they govern. The governed, meanwhile, submit to their leaders, trusting them to conquer the hazards and difficulties confronting society, and at least to know where they are going. As for the machinery of government, the bureaucracy, perhaps it is not out of place to say what Max Weber probably meant, that the structure of bureaucracies and the attitudes of bureaucrats have become more rational by comparison with previous centuries; but it is hardly appropriate to claim, as Max Weber actually did, that contemporary bureaucracy *is* a rational form of organization and that the behaviour of its officials *is* rational behaviour. That is highly misleading. For example, to mention but one aspect, bureaucracy tends to reduce complex social interdependencies to single administrative departments, each with its own strictly defined area of jurisdiction, and staffed by hierarchies of specialists and oligarchies of administrative chiefs who rarely think beyond their own areas of command. This kind of bureaucracy is far closer in character to a traditional organization which has never been properly thought out, than to a clearly thought-out, rational organization whose suitability for its function is constantly under review.

This will have to suffice. With the aid of such examples, certain central sociological concerns may perhaps be seen more clearly. The fact that human societies are made up of human beings, of ourselves, leads us to forget all too easily that their development, structures, and functions are no less unknown to us than the development, structures and functions of the physico-chemical and biological planes. And it is just as important that there should be gradually increasing understanding of all planes. Our contacts with each other are so ordinary and everyday that they can easily mask the fact that at present we ourselves are the least explored subject of research; we are as blank a space on the map of human knowledge as the poles of the earth or the face of the moon. Many people are afraid of exploring this region further, just as people used to fear scientific discoveries about the human organisms. And, just as before, a few argue that the scientific investigation of people by people – something they do not want – is simply not possible. But as men, lacking any more solidly founded understanding of the dynamics of the interweavings they form with each other, drift helplessly from small to ever greater acts of self-destruction, and from one lapse into meaninglessness to the next, so romantic ignorance loses much of its charm as a licence for dreams.

1 Sociology – the questions asked by Comte

Whether they are sociologists or not, people who approach with preconceived ideas the works of the great men who during the nineteenth century were developing a science of society deprive themselves of a great intellectual heritage. It is worthwhile to separate any of their ideas which can still be used in an endeavour to build up a scientific analysis of societies, from those of their ideas which were merely expressions of the transient values of the age. While our conception of the Marxian heritage has been distorted all too often by hatred or eulogy, Auguste Comte (1798–1851), who was the first to designate the word 'sociology' as the express title of the new science, has had much less limelight.

The impression of the legacy of Comte which haunts the textbooks is of some dusty old museum-piece. And indeed we can cheerfully leave a considerable part of his writings to gather dust. He wrote too much. His style was often pompous. He had obsessions, like the notion that all things of significance are tripartite – and he was very likely a little mad. Yet if we put aside the fads and eccentricities and trouble to blow away the dust, we encounter ideas in Comte's work which are virtually new, that have been partially forgotten or misunderstood, and are in their own way no less important for the development of sociology than those of Marx – who would turn in his grave if he knew that he and Comte could even be mentioned in the same breath. But the disparity between their political attitudes and ideals should not be allowed to form a stumbling block. They are not the issue here. Comte was a great man, to put it categorically, and the discrepancy between the problems with which he was actually concerned and the ideas usually ascribed to him is in many instances quite astounding. It is not always easy to find the reasons for this discrepancy, and no attempt to do so will be made here. Comte did far more to assist the development of sociology than simply giving it a name. Like every thinker, Comte built on

B

what others had achieved before him. We will spare ourselves
the details about which ideas Comte took over from Turgot,
Saint-Simon and others, and which of his ideas were 'completely
original'. No one can start from scratch; everyone must start
where others left off. Comte defined a whole series of questions
more clearly than his predecessors. He shed new light on quite a
number of questions. Many of them are as good as forgotten now,
although they are of great scientific significance. From their
neglect, we can infer that science does not progress in a straight
line.

Comte is considered to be not only the father of sociology, but
also the founder of philosophical positivism. His first great work,
which appeared in six volumes between 1830 and 1842, was called
Cours de philosophie positive. The word 'positive' was used by
Comte as a synonym for 'scientific', by which he meant the
acquisition of knowledge by means of theories and empirical
observations.[1] Comte has come to be called a 'positivist'. That is
usually taken to mean an advocate of that theory of science which
holds that scientific work and cognition can be based on observation alone, from which theories are subsequently constructed.
Among the remarkable distortions that Comte's ideas have
suffered is that he was a positivist in this sense. From time to
time people make fun of the naïvety of this kind of 'crude
positivism'. They wonder how anyone can possibly imagine that
observations can be made unless there is already a theory for
determining the selection of things to be observed and a definition
of the problem that one hopes to answer by means of observation. Yet no one has ever emphasized more explicitly and consistently than Comte himself the interdependence of theory and
observation as the core of all scientific work.

For, if on the one hand any positive theory must necessarily be based
on observation, it is equally true on the other that, in order to make
observations, our minds require a theory of some sort. If, in considering phenomena, we did not relate them immediately to some principles,
not only would it be impossible for us to connect these isolated
observations, and in consequence to make any sense of them, but we
should be quite incapable of remembering them; and, most often, the
facts would remain unperceived.[2]

The constant interplay of these two mental operations directed at
theoretical synthesis and at empirical particulars, is one of

Comte's major theses. He was anything but a positivist in the sense of present-day usage; he did not believe that scientific work could proceed by pure induction from observation of particular things, forming comprehensive theories based on the particular observations as almost an afterthought to them. Comte denied this notion as energetically as he contradicted the assertion that a scientific investigation could proceed from pure theories formulated without reference to facts, or from hypotheses posed in the first instance entirely arbitrarily and speculatively, only later being checked against particular facts. Comte had good reasons for breaking so decisively with a philosophical tradition in which people had sought again and again to prove that one of these mental operations must take precedence over the other. For centuries deductionists and inductionists, rationalists and empiricists, apriorists and positivists, or whatever they called themselves, had argued against each other with unabated obstinacy. It is a *Leitmotiv* of Comte's theory of science that scientific work rests upon an indivisible combination of interpretation and observation, of theoretical and empirical work.

His repeated emphasis on the *positive, scientific* nature of all research is explained by the fact that he, as a scientifically trained philosopher, turned with great determination against the philosophy of the preceding centuries. He particularly rejected that of the eighteenth century, the representatives of which permitted themselves to assert propositions without substantiating them by systematically relating them to observations. Many of these propositions were formulated in such a way that they simply could not be tested against observed facts. Comte's choice of the name 'positive' for his philosophy expressed his conscious rejection of this speculative philosophy, which was unrelated to scientific work and did not advance in a scientific manner. The distorted picture of Comte as an 'arch-positivist', using the word in a sense that is diametrically opposed to his actual opinions, demonstrates unconscious revenge on the part of those philosophers who continued to work within the old traditions. Though Comte's proposed solutions did not always succeed; though his constant struggle to express new concepts in old modes of speech often makes it difficult for us to understand those new ideas in retrospect; and though incompetent and incomprehensible translation has further obscured Comte's work, the way he defined problems emerges from his work still fresh, still fruitful.

Three of the problems which Comte posed and tried to solve in his *Philosophie positive* are of particular importance in an introduction to sociology. Comte attempted

(1)   to develop a sociological theory of thought and science;

(2)   to determine the relationship between the three most important groups of sciences on his horizon – the physical, the biological and the sociological;

(3)   to establish within the framework of this system of sciences the relative autonomy of sociology from physics and biology – an autonomy based firmly on the differing nature and scope of their subject matter – and to determine the methods of procedure best suited to sociology.

His formulation of all these problems is closely connected with a fundamental insight common to many thinkers of his day: that social change could not be explained simply in terms of the purposes and actions of individual people, and certainly not only those of princes and rulers. The task was therefore to develop instruments of thought which would enable people to recognize that processes they were gradually beginning to perceive as relatively impersonal could be expressed theoretically as just that. The only categories and concepts then available as a model for this purpose originated in the physical and biological sciences. Accordingly, for a long time people inadvertently took many tools of thought which had been developed to solve problems in biology and physics, and used them to solve sociological problems; this still happens today. But beyond that, they were unable to distinguish clearly between 'nature', in the older sense of the natural sciences, and the new processes then gradually being discovered, which we now call 'society'. In this respect, Comte made the decisive step forward. As a student and later as a tutor and examiner at the famous *Ecole Polytechnique*, he acquired a more thorough education in science and mathematics than most of the men of his time who were concerned with problems of social theory. He realized more clearly than his predecessors that the scientific investigation of society could not be conducted in the same way as a natural science, as if it were another kind of physics. It is often mentioned that Comte invented the name 'sociology' for the new science. *But the reason why he invented a new name for it was that he realized that the science of society was a new kind of science*, which could not be brought under the same conceptual umbrella as physics or biology. Comte's decisive step forward was in recognizing the relative autonomy of the science of society *vis à vis* the older sciences. Giving a new name to the new science gave clear expression to this decisive insight.

Comte saw the main function of the new science as the detection of law-like regularities in social development. To him, as to many other nineteenth century thinkers, the basic problem centred on the urgent questions posed to the intellectual élites by the course of social development and the position within it of the rising bourgeoisie and working class. Where are we going? Where is the development of mankind leading us? Is it moving in the 'right direction', and is that the direction of my own aims and ideals? The way in which Comte tackled these questions betrays an old dilemma which has always confronted philosophers. To themselves, and to others, they appear to be specialists in thought. Therefore their thoughts often revolve around the human mind, the human ability to think, human reason as the key to all aspects of humanity. Rather like Hegel – only without the metaphysical mode of expression – Comte saw the evolution of thought sometimes as only *one* of the key problems and sometimes as *the* key problem in the development of mankind.

Marx was the first to break away from this tradition with any real resolution. In this respect, Comte remained steadfastly within the philosophical tradition. Yet, to one who examines the problem more closely, it is clear that on three decisive points he did break with the philosophical tradition. His break had consequences which are not fully realized even today, because Comte himself often only sketched them briefly and in somewhat antiquated language. But the start he made is enormously significant for the development of sociology and for the philosophy of science.

From a philosophical to a sociological theory of knowledge

The classical theory of knowledge and science examines what happens when the 'subject', a solitary individual, thinks, perceives, and performs scientific work. Comte broke with this tradition. It seemed to him to be at odds with the observable facts. Human thought and research are much more a continuous process, extending over generations. The way in which an individual person goes about thinking, perceiving, or performing scientific work is grounded in the thought processes of previous generations.

In order to understand and explain how people set about these activities, we must therefore also examine this long-term social process of the development of thought and knowledge. The transition from a philosophical to a sociological theory of knowledge, which Comte accomplished, is chiefly apparent in the replacement of the individual person by human society as the 'subject' of knowledge. If questions concerning thought were for him still central to the problems of sociology, he had nevertheless 'sociologized' our conception of the thinking subject.

From non-scientific to scientific knowledge

In classical European philosophy, 'rational' thought – which finds its clearest expression in the natural sciences – is seen as the normal type of thought for all human beings. That this type of thought only appeared late in mankind's development, and that for much of that period of development people did not strive after knowledge in a scientific manner, have remained unacknowledged in the classical theories of knowledge and of science. Indeed they were discarded as irrelevant to any such theory. *For Comte, the problem of the relationship between scientific and non-scientific forms of knowledge became a central question.* It is characteristic of his sociological attitude that he did not judge prescientific thought primarily by its validity, but regarded it simply as a social fact. It is an observable fact, he said, that all scientific knowledge arises out of non-scientific ideas and knowledge. He formulated this insight as a law-like regularity of social development.

. . . each of our principal ideas, each branch of our knowledge, passes successively through three different theoretical stages: the theological or speculative stage; the metaphysical or abstract stage; and the scientific or positive stage. In other words the human mind, by its very nature, uses successively in each of its fields of inquiry three methods of philosophizing . . . first the theological, next the metaphysical, and lastly the positive method.[3]

Human thought and knowledge can be seen in two ways, using different conceptual frameworks. In the first, the conception is of individual people, each of whom – on his own initiative and without prompting – conceives of nature as a blind, automatic, aimless and purposeless mechanism, which nevertheless functions in accordance with theoretical principles. If one rejects this conception, as did Comte, and regards human knowledge as the end-product of a process of development that has spanned hundreds, perhaps even thousands of generations, one can hardly help wanting to know how the scientific pursuit of knowledge is related to the prescientific. Comte attempted a classificatory typology of the stages of mankind's development. In it, he pointed out that people reflect at first on inanimate nature, then on animate nature, and finally on societies. Their reflections were at first always based on speculation, on the quest for absolute, conclusive, dogmatic answers to all their questions, and on a yearning to explain all events of emotional significance to them in terms of the actions, aims and purposes of certain creators, always thought of as people. During the metaphysical phase, explanations in terms of personal creators are replaced by explanations taking the form of personified abstractions. Here Comte had particularly in mind the eighteenth-century philosophers who used personified abstractions like 'Nature' or 'Reason' to explain many events. When people finally reach the positive or scientific stage of thought in a particular branch of knowledge, they cease to search for absolute origins or destinations; while these may well have great personal and emotional significance, they are quite unsupported by observation. The aim of knowledge becomes to find out relationships between actual events. As we might express it nowadays, theories are models of observable relationships. Comte himself, in accordance with the state of knowledge in his time, still spoke of the 'laws' governing these relationships. Instead, we would use terms such as law-like regularities, structures, and functional relationships.

For subsequent work, however, the problem formulated by Comte is more significant than his proposed solution to it. A sociological theory of knowledge and science cannot bypass the questions of how prescientific types of thought and knowledge have developed into scientific ones and of what overall processes of social transformation form the context for this development. Asking questions like this breaks through boundaries fixed hitherto by the orthodox sociology of knowledge, as well as by the philosophical theory of knowledge. The classical sociology of knowledge limited itself to attempting to demonstrate the connections of prescientific ideas or ideologies with social structures. Writers who have worked out connections between certain ideas and the particular social situation of those who uphold them, have always tended to take a relativistic view of those ideas, and to be convinced of their scientific invalidity as mere 'ideologies'. The circularity of this argument can be broken by inquiring into the overall social changes during which prescientific ways of acquiring knowledge have been replaced by scientific ones. Comte's 'law of three stages' indicated among other things the possibility of viewing the development of ideas and modes of thought in the context of wider social changes, and not simply discarding them as false prescientific ideologies. Comte pointed out this whole group of questions; he did not answer them. Yet he drew attention to one aspect of the relationship between scientific and prescientific forms of knowledge, which is of considerable significance for understanding the development of thought, of all the concepts we use, and last but not least of languages. He showed that the genesis of a scientific type of knowledge is scarcely conceivable, except on the foundation of what he called the theological type of knowledge, and which we should perhaps simply call religious. Comte's explanation of this shows how little he was a 'positivist'. People, explained Comte, must make observations in order to construct theories. But they must also possess theories to enable them to make observations.

... the human mind was at first trapped in a vicious circle, from which it would never have had any means of escape, if a natural way out of the difficulty had not fortunately been found by the spontaneous development of theological conceptions.[4]

Here Comte touched on a fundamental aspect of human development.

Let us imagine ourselves back in time when society's store of knowledge was very much smaller. In order to orientate themselves people need a comprehensive picture, a kind of map, to show them how the individual phenomena they perceive are related to each other. Nowadays we know from our own store of experiences that theories, which show how individual events are related to each other, are most useful for orientation and for enabling people to control events, when they are developed with constant feedback from observations. People in earlier times, however, simply did not then have the experience which would have enabled them to know that systematic observation could teach them more about relationships between events. Nonetheless, models of these relationships are indispensable for orientating people to their world. So they constructed what we should now call theories, based on what Comte described as man's spontaneous ability to form images of the relationships between events by means of imagination and fantasy. This explanation, given by Comte in his law of three stages, underlines once more the fruitfulness of a theory of knowledge grounded in a developmental sociology. It is a beginning; it needs to be examined more carefully; but the intellectual model outlined here is certainly worthy of more attention than it has received up to now.

The scientific investigation of the sciences

The philosophical tradition of epistemology and its attendant theory of science rest on a hypothesis about the relationship between the form and the content of thought; or, expressed differently, between the categories and the ingredients of knowledge, or between scientific method and the objects of science. This hypothesis has been handed down from generation to generation and unquestioningly accepted as self-evident. It states that the 'form' of human thought is eternal and unchangeable, however much the contents may change. This assumption runs like an unbroken thread through many discussions of the philosophical theory of knowledge. It is assumed that a science is identified by its use of a particular method, not by the specific character of its subject matter. *Comte turned resolutely against this separation of form from content, of scientific method from scientific subject matter, and of thought from knowledge.* A distinction can be made, he implied, but not a division.

The method must be varied so greatly in its application and modified so comprehensively to correspond in every instance with the specific nature and the complexity of the phenomena, that all general conceptions of method as such would be too vague to be useful. In the simpler branches of the sciences, method and theory are not separate: let us then refrain from separating them when we study the complex phenomena of social life. . . . Therefore I did not try to give an account of the methodology of sociology until I had dealt with science as such.[5]

Comte referred here to a problem which has since been totally shelved once again: the question of how forms of thought are related to knowledge. There is evidence enough that human know-

ledge alters as it develops, and that it has grown, encompassing
wider and wider areas of experience with greater reliability and
adequacy. We need only consider the growing and increasingly
comprehensive control people are able to exercise over the
sequences of events which impinge on them. Yet, even today,
people generally imagine that though knowledge may indeed
change and grow, there is still an eternal, immutable law underlying the human capacity for thought. Our distinction between
the *eternal form* of thought and its *changing contents* is not, however, based on an investigation of the true facts of the case.
Rather, it stems from the human need for security – the need to
discover something absolute and immutable beneath the changing
surface. Many concepts and habits of thought, deeply rooted in
European languages, lend support to the impression that one
thought process is natural, necessary, most fruitful, and applicable
to all problems, especially scientific problems. That is the process
of mentally reducing everything observed as variable and changeable to an absolutely immutable state. Closer observation shows
that the tendency to refer everything changing back to something
unchangeable has to do with an unquestioned value judgement,
which Comte diagnosed as a symptom of a theological mode of
thought. It is taken as self-evident that something which is immutable itself and which can be detected in or behind all change,
is more valuable than change itself. This value judgement is
expressed in the philosophical theory of knowledge and science –
in the idea that there are eternal forms of thought, represented by
'categories' or rules which we call 'logic', underlying all interpersonal communication of ideas, both oral and written, through
the ages.

Here as elsewhere, the idea that supposedly immutable rules of
logic are indeed regular patterns found in all human thought,
rests upon the unheeded confusion of facts with values. Aristotle,
who gave the concept of logic its monumental significance, understood it essentially to mean rules of argument, instructions as to
how arguments in philosophical disputations should be constructed, and how an opponent's mistakes could be demonstrated.
The idea that 'logic' should be a proof of the existence of eternal
laws of thought seems not to have been associated with the
Aristotelian heritage until the late Middle Ages or even after that.
When people use the word 'logical' nowadays, they frequently
confuse one assertion – that the laws of logic are eternal and

universally applicable – with another assertion, that these laws have been the basis of people's thought as actually observable in every society and every age. The same is true of the assertion that there is only one single scientific method. Here too a precept and an ideal are represented as a fact. The transition from a philosophical to a sociological theory of knowledge and science initiated by Comte was based among other things on Comte's displacing from the centre of the theory the question of how a science ought to be conducted. He rather concerned himsef with working out what the distinctive characteristics of scientific procedure actually are, these characteristics distinguishing scientific from prescientific thought. Only on the basis of such a 'positive' or scientific examination of what the sciences can achieve, and on the basis of scientific research taking the sciences themselves as its subject matter, can a scientific theory of the sciences be constructed. Proceeding along these lines, it is soon seen that the view that a particular scientific method, usually that of physics, can be applied to all other sciences as a perpetually valid model, is an expression of a particular value judgement. In cases like this, philosophers set themselves up as judges who decide how one must conduct one's work to pass as a scientist. Hitherto, as Comte pointed out, the autonomous development of sociology has been hindered by this philosophical blend of fact and value, which sets the seal on the method used in a single special science – classical physics – as the quintessence of scientific method.

The traditional philosophical approach to problems is egocentric, in that it limits itself to the question of how an individual can gain scientific knowledge. However, the 'immutable laws of thought' which crop up in classical philosophy are to be understood as the result of a social development of thought and knowledge lasting thousands of years. If they are seen in this light, the question also arises whether there is any factual justification for the traditional distinction between forms of thought, conceived to be invariable, and the variable contents of knowledge. Certainly it is one of Comte's achievements that he abandoned this naïvely egocentric philosophical tradition, orientated towards natural scientific thought; he recognized that prescientific thought, in which people connect individual events in a different way, was an essential precursor, a necessary precondition of scientific thought. Probably he went too far in assuming that, in conformity with his law of three stages, prescientific forms of thought must necessarily develop into scientific forms. That is more likely to be conditional on the direction of overall social development. But Comte was certainly not going too far in stating that all scientific forms of thought must have arisen out of prescientific forms. These prior forms, which he called theological or metaphysical, were the primary and most spontaneous modes of thought for mankind even if not the most adequate and reality-orientated ones. This insight heralds another 'Copernican revolution'. Yet the fact is that more than a hundred years later, Comte's views have hardly ever been echoed, and never taken up, developed and brought to the notice of wider social circles as components of sociological knowledge. This demonstrates what difficulties stood, and still stand, in the way of the fulfilment of this resolution.

People once found it self-evident that the Earth rested, motionless and changeless, at the centre of the universe. Now many people find it self-evident that their own modes of thought are the immutable modes of thought for the whole of mankind. This idea is constantly reinforced by their own experience; these scientific, 'rational' modes of thought prove themselves valid again and again in empirical research and in practical application to the technicalities of everyday life. They seem so unmistakably the 'right' modes of thought that it must seem to the individual that they were a gift from nature, in the form of 'commonsense' or 'reason' – something quite independent of his own upbringing in a particular society or of the development of that society. People cannot remember, and are not taught, how difficult it was for their own society to develop scientific modes of thought out of prescientific ones, and for the scientific modes to achieve ascendancy in all social strata. This was achieved by further development of stocks of thought and knowledge which had first been accumulated by many other human societies. But people are not aware of the special and total social changes which were necessary in European countries to enable them to complete the breakthrough to scientific thought, at first in connection with natural phenomena. Therefore everyone instinctively interprets his own 'rational' ideas about and attitudes towards natural events as a self-evident natural endowment. People automatically took it to be a sign of weakness or inferiority when they found people in other societies whose attitudes to natural forces were still chiefly influenced by prescientific magico-mythical ideas.

The way Comte formulated his ideas may impede our utilizing

the breach he tried to make in the fortress of the old philosophy, or finally our razing its walls to the ground. The sequence of types of thought which he, conforming to the intellectual custom of the age, called a 'law', can be understood more readily if the development of thought structures in a certain direction *is itself seen as an aspect of the development of social structures*. Comte was perfectly well aware of this, for he talked about the connection between the dominance of magico-mythical modes of thought and government by military and priestly strata, and about the connection between prevalence of scientific modes of thought and domination by industrial strata. Since his time, the fund of sociological knowledge about the development of human society has so increased that it would not be difficult to do greater justice to the differentiation and complexity of such connections.

Sociology as a relatively autonomous science

Comte demonstrated, and partially explained, the fact that the subject matter of sociology is *sui generis*, and cannot be reduced to structural peculiarities of human biology – or to use Comte's term, physiology. *It was the insight into the relative autonomy of the subject matter of 'sociology' which was the decisive step forward towards establishing sociology as a relatively autonomous science*. The problem is still topical. Even today, attempts are still made to reduce the structure of social processes to biology or psychology. So it is worthwhile to take a look at the way a man like Comte fought this misconception more than 130 years ago.

In all social phenomena, one first observes the influence of the laws of individual physiology, and beyond that, something special which modifies their effects and which pertains to the influence of individuals on one another, singularly complicated in the human species by the influence of each generation on that which follows it. It is therefore evident that, in order to study social phenomena properly, one must begin with a thorough knowledge of the laws of the individual organism. On the other hand, this necessary subordination between the two studies does not oblige us to regard sociology as simply an appendage of physiology, as some leading physiologists have been led to believe. . . . For it would be impossible to treat the study of mankind collectively as a pure deduction from the study of the human individual, because social conditions which modify the effects of physiological laws are precisely the most essential consideration here. Thus sociology must be based on a body of direct observations appropriate to itself, though taking account where proper of its necessarily intimate relationship with physiology in the narrow sense.[6]

Many of the expressions Comte used have since altered in meaning. The expression 'the human species' (sometimes translated 'human race') has a distinctly biological flavour nowadays. Comte used it without this connotation as a synonym for 'mankind', which in turn meant the same to him as society.

The intellectual difficulty with which he struggled was due to his trying to expound the inseparability of the study of human societies from the study of human biological features, yet at the same time trying to establish the relative autonomy of the former from the latter. With the experience and new tools of thought which have become available, this relationship is now easier to express. For some time, there has been an increasingly widespread understanding in biological circles of specific types of organization, within which a hierarchy of interdependent levels of coordination and integration functions in such a way that relationships at the more complex levels of coordination and integration are relatively autonomous with respect to the less comprehensive levels. The more comprehensive levels of integration are in substance no more than a combination of figurations of the less comprehensive levels, which to a certain extent they regulate. But the way in which the higher levels of integration function is relatively autonomous with respect to their component factors.

Activity at a lower level is always determined by activity at a higher level, but coordination is relatively autonomous at each level. . . . It is the principle of the relative autonomy of each particular level of coordination and integration within this hierarchical schema which has recently received special attention.[7]

As set out here, this insight refers only to the structure of organisms. But as an intellectual model it is of the greatest help in understanding the relationships between the fields of inquiry of the various types of sciences. The sciences of physics, biology and sociology are concerned with differing levels of integration in the cosmos. Here too, types of relationship, structures and regularities are encountered on every level which cannot be explained or understood in terms of those on the preceding level of integration. Thus the functioning of the human organism cannot be explained or understood only in terms of the physico-chemical characteristics of its component atoms; nor can the functioning of a state, a factory or a family be understood just in terms of the biological and psychological characteristics of its individual members. Comte unequivocally recognized the autonomy of particular groups of sciences within the whole system of sciences. He recorded this insight, but did not verify it with the help of empirical research and theoretical models. For him, the insight was still intuitive in character; but the problem had been stated. The task now is to find a more convincing solution. As will be seen, the following chapters devote consider-able attention to this task. We need to show how and why the interweaving of interdependent individuals forms a level of integration at which forms of organization, structures and pro-cesses cannot be deduced from the biological and psychological characteristics of the constituent individuals.

The problem of scientific specialization

Lastly we must mention another of Comte's insights, which anticipated two of the most pressing problems of our time. Per-haps it is surprising that at the beginning of the nineteenth century a man should have been anxious about the consequences of increasing scientific specialization, and should have con-sidered deeply what could be done to obviate the difficulties he foresaw in connection with it. It cannot be regarded as a coincidence that pioneers of sociology, like Comte and Spencer, were concerned with a problem in the theory of science to which the philosophical theory of science paid little attention. Ulti-mately the difference in attitude is due to the sociological theory of science directing research towards the sciences as social facts, while in the philosophical theory of science the factual picture becomes merged with an ideal one. Here it is rewarding to read Comte's own formulation of the problem: it has lost little of its topicality.

In the primitive stage of our knowledge, there exists no regular division among our intellectual endeavours; all the sciences are culti-vated simultaneously by the same minds. This mode of organization of human studies, at first inevitable and even essential, . . . changes little by little, in proportion to the development of the different classes of concepts. By a law, the necessity of which is obvious, each branch of the scientific system gradually grows away from the trunk, as soon as it has grown enough to constitute a distinct discipline. That means when it has reached the point of permanently being able to claim all the attention of a few intellects. It is to this division of the various sorts of learning between different groups of experts that we evidently owe the remarkable development in each of the distinct branches of knowledge at the present day. This has made it manifestly impossible for modern men to equal the polymathic knowledge of all the specialized disciplines which was so easy and common in former times. In short, the intellectual division of labour, carried further and further, is one of the most important and characteristic attributes of the positive philosophy.

But, while recognizing the prodigious results of this division of labour, and while seeing that it is now the true foundation of the general organization of the learned world, it is, on the other hand, impossible not to be struck by the disadvantages now produced by the excessive specialization of the ideas which occupy the exclusive attention of each individual intellect. This unfortunate effect is no doubt to some extent inevitable, and inherent in the very principle of the division of labour. No matter what we do, we shall never be able to equal the omniscience of our forbears, who owed such superiority chiefly to the limited development of their knowledge. Nevertheless, it seems to me that there are appropriate means by which we can avoid the most pernicious effects of exaggerated specialization, without detriment to the invigorating influence of the separation of disciplines. . . . Everyone agrees that the divisions established among the various branches of science for the greater perfection of our efforts, are in the end artificial ones. Let us not forget, despite this agreement, that there are already very few intellects in the learned world who concern themselves with the whole even of a single science, which in turn is still only one of many sciences. Most already confine themselves entirely to the isolated consideration of one more or less extensive section of an established science, without paying much attention to the relation of these particular endeavours to the general system of positive sciences. Let us hurry to remedy this evil, before it becomes more serious. *Let us take care that the human mind does not end up lost in a welter of detail.* We must not deceive ourselves – this is the essentially weak side on which the supporters of theological and metaphysical philosophy can attack the positive philosophy with some hope of success.

The correct means of arresting the harmful influence of the overspecialization of individual research, which threatens the intellectual future, would obviously not be to return to that former confusion of efforts. That would tend to make the human mind regress, and besides it has fortunately become impossible today. On the contrary, the solution consists in perfecting the division of labour itself. All that is necessary is to make the study of science in general one more great speciality. We need a new, appropriately educated class of intellectuals which would, without giving itself up to the special study of any particular branch of natural philosophy, concern itself entirely with the various positive sciences in their present state, with precisely defining the nature of each of them, and with revealing how they are linked, and related to each other. . . . At the same time, other scientists, before giving themselves up to their respective specialities, would in future receive some instruction in the general principles of the positive sciences. This would enable them to profit immediately from the insights gained by the experts devoted to the general study of science. And, in turn, the specialists would be able to correct the generalists' results. This is the state of affairs which scientists are at present visibly approaching day by day.[8]

2 The sociologist as a destroyer of myths

Today sociology itself is in danger of fragmenting into ever more specialist sociologies – from the sociology of the family to the sociology of industrial organizations, from the sociology of knowledge to the sociology of social change, from the sociology of crime to the sociology of art and literature, from the sociology of sport to the sociology of language. Soon there will actually be specialists in all these fields, elaborating their own technical terms, theories and methods which will be inaccessible to non-specialists. Then they will have achieved the ultimate ideal of professionalism – the absolute autonomy of their new speciality. The fortress will be complete, the drawbridges raised. This process has been repeated over and over again during the development of the present-day social sciences – psychology, history, anthropology, economics, political science and sociology, to name but a few.

If we are to explain what sociology is we cannot fail to make mention of this process. It is still taken for granted. People hardly question the increasing division of labour in the field of the social sciences in general and sociology in particular. They are not sufficiently detached from the problems created by increasing scientific specialization to be able to investigate them systematically and scientifically.

That was the possibility Comte was trying to indicate. To deal with problems of this kind, a new type of scientific specialist is required, entrusted with the investigation of long-term social processes like the increasing differentiation of scientific work and its social driving forces. As Comte said, there is obviously a whole series of social factors inhibiting the development of scientific investigation of the sciences. Since his day, scientific specialization has continued, in a way that still remains socially inexplicable and uncontrollable – as if it were a process running wild. Yet, because specialization has increased so much, we are now in a better position to see the extent of the problems raised by such a 'second degree' specialist science. We can now see how such a scientific

investigation of the sciences differs from prescientific philosophical attempts at a theory of science.

Philosophical studies of the sciences implicitly – and sometimes
also explicitly – make it their task to determine, on the basis of
certain given principles, how a science should be conducted.
These principles are very closely connected with the idea, taken
over from theology, that the aim of science is to make eternally
valid pronouncements or to promulgate absolute truths. This is,
as we have said, an imaginary picture of science, based upon a
long-standing theological and philosophical tradition; it is applied
to the sciences as a preconceived dogma, a partially implicit moral
postulate. People do not find it necessary to test by empirical
investigation whether or not this dogmatic hypothesis corresponds
with what scientists actually do. For example, John Stuart Mill
(1806–73) seemed to believe that the inductive process had
primacy over the deductive, so that proceeding from the particular
to the general was superior to proceeding from the general to the
particular. Present-day philosophers like Karl Popper seem more
inclined to acknowledge the primacy of deduction over induction.
But all this is only meaningful as long as one starts out from the
unreal notion that the purpose of the theory of science is to
decide how a person has to proceed in order that his procedure
may be acknowledged as scientific in character. The philosophical
theory of science rests upon a false conception of the problem.

The decisive criterion by which the work of a single scientist
can be actually assessed seems to be his contribution to the
progress of scientific knowledge. Today, the concept of 'progress'
has come into disrepute. It was a central tenet of the bourgeois
intelligentsia of eighteenth- and nineteenth-century Europe; many
intellectuals then adhered to the belief that overall social development was striving relentlessly in the direction of improving the
quality of life. Among their successors this belief has fallen into
disrepute. As a criterion of overall social development, or as an
expression of dogmatic conviction, the concept of progress is
indeed useless. But as an expression of the way scientists themselves evaluate results of their research, it gets to the heart of the
matter.

It is difficult to say whether 'eternal truths', valid for all time,
are embodied in Einstein's theory of relativity, the discovery of
the cholera bacillus, or the development of three-dimensional
models of the atomic structure of large molecules. Traditional

concepts like 'eternal truth' embody unspoken values, themselves standing in need of justification. Basically they are of an edifying nature. In the midst of transience, it is certainly comforting to have something which one can believe to be imperishable. Edifying ideas have their place in human life, but the theory of science is not the place for them. Anyone who, under the pretext of saying what science is, is really saying what he thinks it ideally should be, is deceiving both himself and other people. It is an abuse to talk of a theory of science without having first theoretically assimilated what can be actually observed and tested by scientific study of the sciences.

If this kind of study is undertaken, it is soon discovered that the cause of science has been advanced in certain societies by small groups struggling against untested, prescientific systems of thought. To other and usually far more powerful groups, these latter beliefs appear quite obvious. Scientifically thinking groups are generally groups which criticize or reject the dominant and commonly accepted ideas of their society, even when these are upheld by recognized authorities, for they have found that they do not correspond to the observable facts. *In other words, scientists are destroyers of myths.* By factual observation, they endeavour to replace myths, religious ideas, metaphysical speculations and all unproven images of natural processes with theories – testable, verifiable and correctable by factual observation. Science's task of hunting down myths and exposing general beliefs as unfounded in fact will never be finally accomplished. For both within and beyond groups of scientific specialists, people are always turning scientific theories into belief systems. They extend the theories, and use them in ways divorced from the theoretically directed investigation of facts.

In spite of all this, *progress* is still the criterion by which the results of research are judged, whether on the theoretical or on the empirical level, or on both. What advance do the results represent when measured against current social or, more specifically, scientific stocks of knowledge? This sort of progress has many facets. It may involve adding to the stock of knowledge. It may involve establishing more certainly a piece of knowledge which previously rested on relatively insecure foundations. It may involve embracing within a single theory facts not hitherto known to be connected, or else relating events to each other within a more comprehensive model than earlier theories offered.

It may simply mean that theory and empirical evidence are brought into closer agreement with each other. In each of these cases, it is crucial that criteria such as 'true' and 'false', 'right' and 'wrong', which were decisive in the traditional philosophy of science, have moved from the centre to the periphery of the theory of science. Of course, it is still possible for research findings to be proved absolutely wrong. But in the more developed sciences the main yardstick is the relationship of newer findings to older available knowledge. This is not something which can be expressed in static polarities like 'true' and 'false', but only by demonstrating the difference between old and new; this becomes apparent through the dynamics of scientific processes, in the course of which theoretical and empirical knowledge becomes *more extensive, more correct, and more adequate.*

If a sociological theory of knowledge is to be based not on the postulation of scientific utopias but on the investigation of sciences as observable social processes, then it must focus on the nature of the cognitive processes in the course of which first a few, then more and better organized groups of people succeed in bringing human knowledge and thought into ever closer agreement with an ever more comprehensive range of observable data.

To recognize this task is to break away from both philosophical absolutism and the still widely prevalent sociological relativism. One can step outside the vicious circle which again and again traps people in sociological relativism the moment they have freed themselves from philosophical absolutism, and, should they try to wriggle out of that snare, lands them back in the spurious dogmatic refuge of philosophical absolutism.

So, on the one hand, there is the philosophical theory of knowledge, which takes scientific knowledge for granted. It does not bother about how or why the scientific way of acquiring knowledge arose out of the prescientific. The philosophical problem is posed in terms only of static alternatives, and so prescientific or non-scientific findings and forms of knowledge are bound to be 'wrong' and 'untrue', while the scientific forms are 'right' and 'true'. Accordingly, the philosophical theory of science offers no way of making the actual problems of scientific development central to its concerns. It cannot come to grips with the process by which the relatively undifferentiated research efforts of earlier times have been transformed into ever more specialized processes of research. Even today, in talking about the theory of science, we speak of 'science' and 'the scientific method', as if there were only one science and one scientific method – an idea just as chimerical as the older notion that there is one cure for all illnesses.

Then, on the other hand, there is the sociological theory of science, which deals exclusively with the social determination of prescientific patterns of thought. Just as the philosophical theory of science has almost exclusively taken as its model scientific knowledge of natural events, so the sociological theory of knowledge has so far been concerned almost entirely with ideas about society and with political and social ideologies. It has not asked *how and under what conditions non-ideological, scientific knowledge of natural and social relationships is possible.* Nor have social scientists fully clarified, either for themselves or for others, how and indeed whether sociological theories differ from social ideologies. The prevailing sociology of knowledge, like the philosophical theory of knowledge, neglects the question of what conditions allow prescientific myths and ideologies to develop into scientific theories, either about nature or about society.

The sociological theory of science, which first began to emerge in the work of Comte and is now at last becoming more intelligible, puts these very problems in a position of central importance. It poses a key question. Under what social conditions did people succeed in expanding their knowledge of human societies and in continually reconciling their knowledge with observed facts? It cannot yet be said with certainty that overall social development will necessarily lead to the progressive emancipation of the social sciences as it did for the natural sciences. It is too early to tell; we are still caught up in the process of emancipation. Nevertheless, we can be more sure about the past. The structure of thought began to move in a fairly obvious direction during the period when people were starting to treat social problems more as scientific than as theological or philosophical ones. By examining the process of scientificization of thought and perception in the light of developmental sociology, the structural properties which distinguish the scientific pursuit of knowledge from the prescientific can be theoretically clarified. That is beyond the capacity of the traditional philosophical theory of science, because it is dominated by the fictitious hypothesis that scientific knowledge is the 'natural', 'reasonable', 'normal' or, at any rate, the eternal, unchanging and unchangeable form of human cognition. Consequently it rejects the study of the social origins and development of the sciences as 'merely historical', 'unphilosophical', and therefore irrelevant to a theory of science. Yet observation of this kind, proceeding by a comparative method, is the one way of systematically separating the unscientific and less scientific from the more scientific production of knowledge. In rejecting it, the philosophical approach denies itself the one chance of ascertaining the distinctive structural properties of the scientific pursuit of knowledge, without dragging in arbitrary, preconceived values and ideals.

The development of science has frequently been seen as a subject for merely historical study, whereas science as the object of systematic philosophical investigation has been seen as in an eternal, unchanging state. The approach advocated here avoids this naïve dichotomy. It is neither systematic nor historical in the traditional sense of these concepts. The development of scientific knowledge, whether about 'nature' or 'society', must itself be regarded as a transition to a new phase in the general human quest for knowledge; only then can it be itself investigated and defined theoretically. This development has many aspects and can vary enormously in detail. But it is possible to establish the direction of any such development with some precision. For example, whenever the vocabulary of a society is found to contain concepts expressing ideas about an *impersonal* and to some extent self-regulating and self-perpetuating nexus of events, it is certain that they are descended in unbroken line from other concepts implying a *personal* nexus of events. In every case, the latter was the point of departure. People model their ideas about all their experiences chiefly on their experiences within their own groups. The models of thought people had developed about their own intentions, actions, plans and purposes were not always really suitable either for understanding or manipulating nexuses of events. This is a difficult idea though, and it took a long time and the cumulative and arduous efforts of many generations for people to learn to grasp it. What we now designate as 'nature' has certainly always been a largely self-regulating, self-perpetuating and more or less autonomous set of events; but it was a long time before mankind was in a position to conceive of the endless variety of individual natural events as a random, mechanical and regular system, which no one had either planned or intended. The development of human society, and accordingly of knowledge and thought, was slow and intermittent at first, but quickened in tempo from the Renaissance. How and why people learned to perceive and to interpret nexuses of events in nature in a way very different from their own immediate self-experiences need not concern us at this point.

Comparison with the growth of natural science makes it easier to see precisely what difficulties men have had to combat – and indeed are still combating – in attempting to understand their own social interconnections. Slowly they have come to realize that the structures they form with other people can be better explained and understood if these structures are thought of not simply as congeries of particular individuals known by name, but also as impersonal and to some extent self-regulating, self-perpetuating configurations. *That is not in the least to suggest that social bonds are anything at all like the kind that physicists encounter in their work.* What it does show clearly is that in both cases the transition to scientific modes of thought is connected with a new conception of the nature of particular events. What had previously been experienced without much reflection as a variety of actions, intentions and purposes on the part of particular living beings is now conceived as a distinctive kind of nexus of events. It is experienced in effect with more detachment, as being relatively autonomous, relatively uncontrolled and impersonal. That people are able to perceive a particular nexus of events in this way could be said to be a condition for the transition to scientific modes of thought. To put it another way, it is symptomatic of the transition from prescientific to scientific ways of gaining knowledge that the tools of thought people use should slowly cease to be concepts of *action* and become concepts of *function*. A growing recognition of the relative autonomy of a field of investigation as a special kind of functional nexus is a *prerequisite* of the two operations characteristic of scientific procedure. These are the construction of relatively autonomous theories about the relationships between observable details, and the testing of these theories against systematic observations.

As long as people believe that events are the outcome of the more or less capricious plans and intentions of certain living beings, they cannot suppose it very reasonable to examine problems on the basis of observation. If events are ascribed to supernatural beings or even exalted humans, the 'mystery' can only be resolved by gaining access to the authorities who know about the secret plans and intentions. It is often thought that the transition to scientific types of knowledge depends primarily on a changeover to the use of a particular method of investigation. The idea that people can discover a method or a tool of thought, independently of their conception of the subject matter about which knowledge is to be gained, is, however, a product of the philosophical imagination. It is often assumed, probably quite unthinkingly, that the image of nature as a self-regulating process has always been prevalent, and that all that was needed was the discovery of some method of bringing to light individual examples of regular relationships. In reality, the theoretical conception of a nexus of events and the method of investigating it developed in functional interdependence. It is particularly difficult to develop a relatively autonomous conception of society which can serve as a key to scientific discovery. The reason is that such a conception conflicts not only with prescientific conceptions of *society* but also with prevailing scientific conceptions of nature. Functional interconnections in society are not identical with those at the lower level of integration represented by physical nature. This is not recognized universally. All our ideas about impersonal nexuses of events stem directly from the level of physical nature; from this realm of experience are derived all categories like causality, all tools of thought and methods of investigation which can be employed in understanding such nexuses. Furthermore, the professional groups involved in research in the natural sciences possess particularly great social power and, in consequence, social status. Social scientists, like all upwardly mobile groups, are only too eager to bask in the reflected glory of the older sciences by adopting their prestigious models. Unless this is borne in mind, it is impossible to appreciate why it has taken sociology so long to develop as a relatively autonomous field of investigation.

Remembering all this, we are better able to recognize what can be learned about the structural properties of scientific knowledge by studying the emancipation from the prescientific. Attempts to establish a particular method as the decisive criterion of science do not reach the heart of the matter. Nor is it enough to rely on the recognition that all scientific procedure is based on constantly referring back inclusive intellectual models to particular observations, and these observations back to inclusive intellectual models. What is wrong with such statements is their formal character. Systematic observation only becomes meaningful if people already have a general idea of the field of investigation. Again, the separation of theory and method proves to be based on a misconception. The development of people's conception of the subject matter is found to be inseparable from their conception of the method appropriate to its investigation. At the same time, it is quite understandable that people should feel repugnance at the idea that the society of which they themselves are members is a functional nexus relatively autonomous of the objectives and intentions of its members. Similar resistance was encountered during the period when people were struggling towards the idea that natural events are a blind, purposeless functional nexus. In the immediate aftermath of recognizing this, people often experienced a sense of meaninglessness. 'Is there no purpose?' they used to ask; 'Is there no aim behind the eternal circling of the planets?' To arrive at a conception of nature as a mechanical, regular nexus of functions, people had to free themselves from the much more satisfying idea that behind every natural event there is a purpose of significance to them, the actual motive force. The paradox was that people were unable to take steps against the constant menace of natural events, unable to see meaning and purpose in such precautions, until they were able to perceive the meaninglessness, the purposelessness and the blind mechanical regularity of physical events. In attempting to put over the insight that social processes also are relatively autonomous of human intentions and purposes, the same difficulties and the same paradox constantly recur. Many people find the idea repugnant. It is frightening to realize that people form functional interconnections within which much of what they do is blind, purposeless and involuntary. It is much more reassuring to believe that history – which is of course always the history of particular human societies – has a meaning, a destination, perhaps even a purpose. And indeed there is always a supply of people willing to tell us what that meaning is. Certainly, in the short term, a sense of meaninglessness may be the immediate result of depicting social interconnections in these terms – as relatively autonomous and to some extent self-regulating functional nexuses, unguided by anyone's aims and intentions and not striving towards any of the goals fixed by current values. Yet, in the long run again, people can only hope to master and make sense out of these purposeless, meaningless functional interconnections if they can recognize them as relatively autonomous, distinctive functional interconnections, and investigate them systematically.

So that is the core of the transition to scientific ways of thinking about societies. Frequent reference has been made to the concept of 'relative autonomy'. This refers to three different but completely interdependent aspects of the sciences. First, there is the relative autonomy of the subject matter of a science within the whole universe of interdependent events. Division of the scientific world into a number of different types of sciences, primarily centred on physics, biology and sociology, would very much hamper scientists' work if the division did not correspond to an arrangement of the cosmos itself. Therefore the first level of relative autonomy, and the foundation for the other two, is *the relative autonomy of the subject matter of one science with respect to the subject matter of the other sciences.* The second level is *the relative autonomy of scientific theory about this subject matter.* This means two things. It is no longer closely bound up with prescientific conceptions of its subject matter, couched in terms of purpose, meaning and intention. It is also relatively autonomous in relation to theories about other fields of investigation. The third level is *the relative autonomy of a given science within academic institutions conducting teaching and research.* This also involves the relative autonomy of groups of professional scientists, the specialists in a certain subject, with respect both to groups representing other sciences, and to non-scientists. This social scientific definition of the structural properties of a science is based entirely on the study of what actually exists. It has grown out of the continuing search for knowledge, and can be amended in the light of further investigation, whether theoretical or empirical. But if scientific study of the sciences is limited in this way, its findings will be the more applicable to practical problems. Again and again, groups of scientists try to justify their possession or acquisition of relatively autonomous academic institutions by developing their own theories, methods and technical terms, while the relative autonomy of their theoretical and conceptual apparatus is not justified by the relative autonomy of their subject matter. In other words, side by side with scientific specialization justified by correspondingly separate fields of investigation, there exists a good deal of *pseudo-specialization.*

Unlike the philosophical theory, the sociological theory of science does not hand down laws or decree established principles to dictate which methods are 'valid science' and which are not. What it does do is to keep closely in touch with acute practical issues in the sciences. Using the sociological theory of science as a starting-point, it is possible to investigate how far the customary, institutionalized lines of demarcation between scientific subjects corresponds at any given time to the actual state of knowledge about the arrangement of the various fields of inquiry, and to what extent the development of the sciences has caused discrepancies. All in all, it can be said that philosophical theories of science concentrate on the *one* ideal science and, within that, on the *one* scientific method; as so often in traditional philosophy, the rules of the game place a kind of invisible barrier between the thinker and the object of his thought – in this case, the sciences. Many acute scientific problems, to which much practical effort is given in the real scientific world are, within the framework of the philosophical theory of science, dismissed as philosophically irrelevant. According to the rules of the game, they are beside the point. Matters which seem beside the point according to the philosophical rules are, however, highly relevant to a more reality-orientated theory.

So the common structural features of the scientific acquisition of knowledge cannot be discovered without considering the whole scientific world, taking into account the multiplicity of sciences. The orientation of our conception of science to one particular discipline, for example physics, is roughly equivalent to the way some societies believe that all people look like themselves, and that if they look different they cannot be real people. We must turn away from the restrictive rules of the philosophical study of science, and take the sciences as objects for theoretical and empirical investigation. It will then soon become apparent that the conception of the subject matter, as it emerges in the course of scientific work, is functionally interdependent with the conception of the method used to investigate it. That is understandable. What should we think of someone who maintained that an axe must always be used to shape any material, be it wood, marble or wax? Similarly, the social structure of scientific activity cannot be ignored, though it often seems to be, by anyone who wants to understand the criteria which determine the scientific value of research findings. Progress in each scientific field is partly dependent on the scientific standards and the scientific ethos of those who work in that field. And their competitiveness, whether mild or fierce, their areas of dispute and disagreement ultimately determine whether and to what extent the results obtained by a particular scientist can or cannot be registered as progress, as an advance in scientific knowledge.

The social nature of scientific research is demonstrated by the repeated demand that its findings be 'replicable' and 'testable'. Testability is always understood to mean testable by other people as well as the investigator. Certainly, no scientific method can in itself guarantee the validity of all results obtained by its application. If a researcher's attitudes and scientific criteria are to any extent shaped by heteronomous, extra-scientific considerations, whether political, religious or national – or even considerations of professional status – his efforts may all amount to a waste of time. That kind of thing used to happen more than occasionally in the social sciences, and indeed still happens now. The reason is not hard to discern. Research in the social sciences, not least in sociology, has as yet achieved only a comparatively slight measure of relative autonomy. International and intranational disagreements are so violent and so intense that efforts to increase the autonomy of sociological theories from extra-scientific belief systems have so far met with limited success. At all events, the standards by which specialists in the field judge research are still determined largely by this kind of heteronomous criterion. One reason why people in many of the social sciences cling in a rather formal way to a certain method as proof of their scientific respectability, is very likely that the vehemence of extra-scientific disputes actually prevents them overcoming the problem of ideological influences on scientific activity at both theoretical and empirical levels.

From such reflections, it can be better appreciated that the transition to more scientific ways of thinking about society, which slowly got under way in the late eighteenth century and developed in the nineteenth and twentieth centuries, was an amazing achievement. On the one hand, it is regrettable that sociological theory has not achieved greater autonomy; selection and definition of problems is still entangled with unconsidered, unscientific thinking about social problems. On the other hand, given the intensity of social conflicts at the time, we may well ask how it was possible that people ever emancipated themselves sufficiently from those struggles to make even a first effort towards scientific study of these phenomena.

The rise of sociology can be better understood if it is borne in mind that social conflicts and disputes themselves underwent a peculiar depersonalization during the period of industrialization in the nineteenth and twentieth centuries. There was an increasing tendency for social disputes to be conducted not so much in the name of particular people as in the name of certain impersonal principles and articles of belief. This seems obvious to us, so we often do not realize how strange and unique it was when people in these centuries came to be fighting no longer in the name of ruling princes and their generals, nor in the name of religion, but chiefly in the name of fixed impersonal principles like 'conservatism' and 'communism', 'socialism' and 'capitalism'. At the centre of each of these social belief systems in the name of which people were fighting was the question of how people should organize their lives together in society. Not only from sociology and all the social sciences, but also from the ideas which dominated the struggles in which people were engaged, can it be deduced that at that time people were beginning to think of themselves in a new sense – as societies.

People have evidently often found it very difficult to appreciate what sociologists really mean when they say that the subject matter of their research is human society. So perhaps it may help to explain what sociology is about if we can picture the circumstances in which people arrived at an awareness of themselves as societies – an awareness evinced not only in the form of sociology, but in their extra-scientific disputes too.

The structural change in people's self-awareness found expression in their tendency to fight more and more in the name of great 'isms'; but the change cannot be understood unless it is itself recognized as reflecting certain changes in human social life.

Everyone knows about these changes, yet they are not always perceived clearly and unequivocally as changes in social structure. They are usually labelled 'historical events'. In other words, people perceive a wealth of detail about events in various industrialized countries of Europe during the nineteenth and twentieth centuries. In France there was a revolution. Kings and emperors came and went. Eventually bourgeois and workers' parties fought for and created a republic. In England Reform Acts extended the franchise to the bourgeoisie and the workers, and admitted their representatives to government posts. The power of the House of Lords declined, while that of the House of Commons increased. Eventually England became a country ruled by the industrial bourgeoisie and the industrial workers. In Germany, lost wars contributed to a decline in the power of the dominant dynastic-agrarian-military strata, while people of the former lower strata became more important. Eventually, after many swings of the pendulum, the old assemblies of estates were replaced by parliamentary assemblies of party representatives. The list could be continued. The details are, as we have said, familiar enough. But as yet scientific perception is not sufficiently well organized for the uniform direction of development to be visible in the welter of detail. We cannot see the wood for the trees. We do not probe deeply enough to uncover the real problem. What were the reasons for the transformation of the whole human situation in these and other countries? All were moving in one and the same direction; they had in common increasing scientificization of control over nature, increasing occupational differentiation and many other trends. This is precisely the sociological problem. Until this point has been taken, it is difficult to appreciate what sociologists understand by 'society'. When it has, though, it can be seen that beneath the many differences of historical detail between the various countries, there was a structural parallelism in their overall development as societies.

The rise of sciences committed to the investigation of societies was itself one facet of this phase in the development of state-societies. The episode was distinguished by, among other things, the increasing scientificization of control over nature, seen for example in the discovery of new sources of energy, and in a corresponding advance in occupational differentiation. There was a connection between the incipient trend towards scientificization of thought about society and structural changes within the state-societies where these intellectual transformations occurred. The connection only becomes evident, however, through awareness of the common trend in their overall development just referred to.

These parallels in development escape notice very easily if attention is paid only to one sphere of development, whether it is the economic, the political or the social. That is one of the difficulties. Industrialization, scientificization, bureaucratization, urbanization, democratization or the growth of nationhood – whichever concept is seized upon to demonstrate parallelism in social change, it emphasizes only one particular aspect or another. Our conceptual tools are not yet sufficiently well developed to express the nature of the overall social transformation, nor to explain the connections between its individual aspects.

Yet the sociological problem with which we are here concerned lies in doing just that. The common direction has to be brought to light not just in one sphere but in the all-pervading transformation of human relationships. This can best be achieved – perhaps provisionally – by mentally re-humanizing all the rather de-humanizing concepts used to characterize the development. After all, industrialization ultimately means nothing more than that more and more people came to be occupied as entrepreneurs, employees and workers. Scientificization of control over nature means that more and more people were working as physicists and engineers. Democratization means that the balance of power shifted to some extent in favour of the former 'plebs'. The same is true of the glib way we mentally divide society into 'economic', 'political' and 'social' spheres. These all refer to specific nexuses of functions which people perform for themselves as well as for others. If the political, the economic and all the other 'spheres' are regarded as functional nexuses of interdependent people, it will soon be seen that the division is merely a conceptual one. Moreover, it bears no relation to any sociological model of their interdependence, and so it leads sociological research astray. We need only consider a phenomenon like taxation. Are taxes 'economic', 'social' or 'political' phenomena? Is the decision about how the tax burden should be shared a purely 'economic', purely 'political' or purely 'social' one? Or is it not rather the outcome of a balance of power between various groups of people, between the rulers and the ruled, between richer and poorer strata, which can be fairly precisely determined sociologically?

It will still be some time before we possess easily communicable concepts to facilitate the study of such overall social changes. Here it is sufficient to indicate one central change in the overall figuration of society. A certain shift in the balance of power is among the fundamental common features in the development of most European countries in the nineteenth and twentieth centuries. Government posts came to be filled more and more by representatives of political parties – mass organizations which replaced quite small élites distinguished by inherited property or inherited privilege. Nowadays parties occupy such an obvious place in our social life that even in scientific studies we are usually content to describe and illuminate only their institutional exterior. Efforts are no longer made to explain why in all these societies, oligarchic rule by small privileged dynastic–agrarian–military groups has somehow given way sooner or later to oligarchic rule by parties, whether the regime is multi-party or one-party. What overall change in the structure of each of these societies has caused the ruling strata of previous centuries to decline in power in relation to the social heirs of those who were often referred to as the common herd? As history, all these details are quite well-known, yet beyond the details people do not see at all clearly. They cannot perceive the broad common direction of the transformations within the functional interconnections and figurations people form together. Nor, in consequence, do they see the sociological problems posed by the common direction of development in many state-societies. Their history is in many respects diverse. How is it then that the internal balance of power in each of these countries has nevertheless shifted in much the same direction?

Defining one major problem of developmental sociology may have helped to show what sociology is all about. The origins of sociology cannot be understood apart from this radical transformation of society. Societies oligarchically ruled by the hereditarily privileged were transformed into societies ruled by the recallable representatives of mass political parties. The shift in the internal balance of power is symptomatic of the overall transformation of society. The social sciences, especially sociology, can be said to have the same social parentage as the belief-systems of the great mass parties, the major social ideologies of our age. However disparate social science and social ideology may be, both are manifestations of the same transformations in the structure of society. Here we shall have to limit ourselves to only a brief survey of a few aspects of these connections.

1 *The reduction of power differentials between governments and governed*

The extension of the franchise was the most conspicuous institutional expression of this reduction in power differentials. It usually came about in stages, varying from country to country, though the direction was always the same. Often the franchise was extended first only to the property-owning middle classes, then to all adult males, then to all adults, women as well as men. The view of history which depicts social changes as resulting from specific individual events can easily lead to the conclusion that state legislation to extend the franchise was the cause of the comparative increase in the power of the governed relative to that of governments. But that is putting the cart before the horse. The legal extension of the franchise, often against strong resistance, was the manifest institutional consequence of the latent shift in the distribution of power towards broader strata. In the preceding centuries, access to the central monopoly power chances of the state and influence over appointments to government posts was usually confined to small, dynastic, aristocratic élites. However, the changes in the texture of human relationships which occurred in each of the more developed countries during the nineteenth and twentieth centuries were such that no section of society remained simply a relatively passive object of domination by others. None of them remained entirely without institutional channels through which they could exercise pressure, directly or indirectly, upon governments, and in some cases they could influence appointments to government offices. The emergence of mass political party organizations in the nineteenth and twentieth centuries was simply a manifestation of this limited reduction of the power differentials between governments and governed. Seen from the perspective of our own times, these power differentials certainly remained large enough. Seen in the perspective of the long-term development of societies, however, the chances of the bulk of the governed to exercise a measure of control over governments, relative to the chances of governments to control the governed, became somewhat greater than they had been. Rulers in every country had to legitimize themselves in the eyes of their subjects by means of relatively impersonal principles and ideals concerning the ordering of social conditions. They had to offer their own idealistic programmes for social reorganization as a way of gaining followers and fellow-believers. And they attempted to win over the masses with plans for improving their living conditions. All these were characteristic symptoms of the relative change in the distribution of power between rulers and ruled. From this alone it is plain to see how an increase in interdependence brings about a transformation of thought about society and the formulation of fairly impersonal programmes for the improvement of social conditions. It therefore also leads to the perception of societies as functional nexuses of interdependent people.

2 *The reduction of power differentials between different strata*

Seen in isolation, the differences between the power chances of different strata in the more developed industrial countries are still very great indeed. But viewed in the context of the direction of long-term social development over the last two or three hundred years, they are put in perspective. It is clear that power differentials have diminished, not only between governments and governed, but also between different strata of society. A few centuries ago, noble landowners were very much less dependent on their peasants, and army officers on their mercenary soldiers, than present-day industrialists are on their workers or professional officers on their conscripted citizens in uniform. For the bulk of the population, which used to be virtually powerless, this second development has resulted in an increase in their relative power potentials. Except where the institutionalized balance of domination corresponded to the actual power potentials of the mass, the increase showed itself in diffuse manifestations of discontent and apathy, and in looming rebellion and violence. Provided the society had developed institutional means of assessing the distribution of power and legal methods of making constant adjustments to keep pace with changes in the power ratio, these feelings could find expression through electoral choice, through strikes, and in mass party demonstrations and mass movements, each with its own social belief system. However that may be, in the wake of the overall social transformation usually labelled by one of its aspects such as 'industrialization', there has been a lessening of power differentials between all groups and strata – as long as they remain within the constantly changing functional orbit of the society. This last qualification indicates that again and again in the course of social differentiation and corresponding integration, certain social groups have suffered reductions in the scope of their functions, and even total loss of function; the consequence has been loss of power potential. But the overall trend of the transformation was to reduce all power potentials between different groups, even down to those between men and women, parents and children.

This trend is referred to by the concept of 'functional democratization'. It is not identical with the trend towards the development of 'institutional democracy'. It refers to a shift in the social distribution of power, and this can manifest itself in various institutional forms, for example in one-party systems as well as in multi-party systems.

3 *Transformation of all social relationships in the direction of a greater degree of reciprocal, multi-polar dependence and control*
Central to this whole social transformation have been impulses towards growing specialization or differentiation in all social activities. Corresponding to these have been impulses towards integration of the specialized activities, which has often lagged behind. In this case too, social scientists often pay attention only to the institutional veneer and not to the total structure of society. Thus they talk about 'pluralistic societies', by which they chiefly mean a structural arrangement of institutions subject to self-regulation or government control. But the increased institutional multi-polarity and reciprocal control among various social groups is again only an institutional manifestation of the attenuation of power differentials between all groups and individuals in the course of the transformation. Because of their particular specialized functions, all groups and individuals become more and more functionally dependent on more and more others. Chains of interdependence become more differentiated and grow longer; consequently they become more opaque and, for any single group or individual, more uncontrollable.

4 *Social sciences and social ideals as instruments of orientation when social bonds are relatively opaque and when awareness of their opacity is increasing*
The connection between development of the social sciences and overall social development emerges rather more clearly here. The opacity of social networks to the people who form them by reason of their mutual control and dependence is characteristic of networks at all stages in their development. But only in a particular phase of development could people become aware of this opacity and also, therefore, of uncertainty about themselves as a society. Some of the structural properties of this phase of development have been set out here – properties which enabled people to become aware of themselves as societies, as people who

together form various kinds of functional nexuses and constantly changing figurations. Paramount among them is functional democratization, the narrowing of power differentials and development towards a less uneven distribution of power chances; it permeates the whole gamut of social bonds, although there are impulses simultaneously running counter to this trend. In its turn, this development is connected with the increasing differentiation or specialization of all social activities, and the correspondingly increasing dependence of every person and every group on more and more others. The development of ever longer chains of human interdependence makes it increasingly obvious that it is inadequate to explain social events in pre-scientific terms, singling out individual people as their originators. People experience the increasing opacity and growing complexity of human interweaving. They find that the possibility of any one person, no matter how powerful he may nominally be, taking decisions purely on his own account, independently of other people, is obviously restricted. They witness decisions constantly being made in the course of trials of strength and struggles for power between many people and groups – struggles sometimes conducted strictly according to rule, sometimes less so. All this practical experience forces people to realize that other, more impersonal modes of thought are required if these opaque social processes are to be understood, let alone brought under control. One result of this awakening consciousness of the relative opacity of social processes and the inadequacy of explanations constructed solely in terms of individual people has been an effort to examine social processes using an approach analogous to that of the older sciences. They are treated as internally consistent, largely self-regulating and relatively autonomous functional nexuses; in short, scientific methods are applied. Another result has been that people tend to orientate themselves to relatively opaque social situations with the aid of relatively impersonal but emotionally charged social belief systems and ideals. These are all the more satisfying because they usually promise immediate relief for all social ills and sufferings, or even a complete cure in the near future. The two types of orientation, the scientific and the ideological, have usually developed in close association. The difference between the two types of intellectual orientation in the human world still remains to be worked out in detail. The development of human society still remains opaque and is still beyond our powers of control. Sooner or later we shall consciously have to decide which of the two types of orientation, the scientific type or that based on preconceived social beliefs, is the more likely to succeed in elucidating it and making it more susceptible to control.

3 Game models

Given the present state of sociological thinking, one of the persistent problems of sociology is on what grounds sociologists can claim that they have a field of their own distinct from that of biologists, psychologists, historians and other groups of specialists. For the subject matter of sociology is 'society', and societies are after all nothing but composite units of which individual human beings form the component parts. Is it not therefore necessary for sociologists to rely in the first instance on the findings of all those other disciplines which, like human biology, psychology or history, study individual human beings – the constituent parts of societies as such – and then to see whether they as sociologists have anything to add to the findings of these other disciplines? Would it not, moreover, be best and most obvious for sociologists first to study individual people singly, and then to see whether they can distil from a great mass of such individual studies any generalizations which can be presented as properties of 'societies'?

Quite a number of sociologists do in fact proceed in this manner. They investigate the behaviour, views and experience of individual people and process their results statistically. By means of inquiries of this type, focused on the 'component parts' of societies, they endeavour to bring to light the characteristics of the 'composite units', of the societies themselves. And as some of their findings do in fact indicate social connections and regularities beyond the reach of other disciplines concerned with the study of human beings singly, these sociological findings are often implicitly treated as the solution to the problem of whether or not sociology can claim some kind of autonomy in relation to these other individual-centred social sciences. It is an answer which relies on scientific practice, on success or claimed success in solving empirical problems, rather than on a clear theoretical answer as to why it should be possible for sociologists, by studying the behaviour or experience of individual people, to carve out a special field of inquiry for themselves which is not already covered by other disciplines which also study individual people.

It is quite understandable that many people have believed in the past, and may still believe today, that all things social can and should be explained in terms of the psychological or perhaps even physical characteristics of people. The classical tradition of the physical sciences has been immensely influential. According to that tradition, the way to investigate a composite unit is to dissect it into its component parts, then to study the properties of the component parts in isolation, and finally to explain the distinguishing properties of the composite unit in terms of its component parts. Thus, the properties of molecules may be explained in terms of the properties of atoms, and these in turn in terms of their component particles. But does this method hold good for all fields of investigation? The difficulty is that the tradition of scientific atomism (as we may call it for short) lives on in theory, while scientific practice in many fields has run in a different direction. As has been shown elsewhere in greater detail,[1] the more closely integrated are the components of a composite unit, or in other words the higher the degree of their functional interdependence, the less possible it is to explain the properties of the latter only in terms of the former. It becomes more necessary not just to explore a composite unit in terms of its component parts, but also to explore the way in which these individual components are bonded to each other so as to form a composite unit. The study of the configuration of the unit parts, or in other words the structure of the composite unit, becomes a study in its own right. This is the reason why sociology cannot be reduced to psychology, biology, or physics: its field of study – the figurations of interdependent human beings cannot be explained if one studies human beings singly.[2] In many cases the opposite procedure is advisable – one can understand many aspects of the behaviour or actions of individual people only if one sets out from the study of the pattern of their interdependence, the structure of their societies, in short from the figurations they form with each other.

Some people tend to shrink from this insight. They confuse it with a metaphysical assumption of long standing which is often summed up in the saying 'the whole is more than the sum of its parts'. Using the term 'whole' or 'wholeness' creates a mystery in order to solve a mystery. This aberration must be mentioned because many people appear to believe that one can only be one or the other – either an atomist or a holist. Few controversies are as unattractive as that in which two groups of antagonists run around in circles, each defending its own speculative and untestable thesis by attacking another that is equally speculative and untestable on the grounds that no third alternative is possible. In the case of atomism and holism, it most certainly is.

How exactly does it come about that people, because of their interdependence and the way their actions and experience intermesh, form a type of figuration, a kind of order which is relatively autonomous from the type of order encountered if, like biologists or psychologists, one investigates individual people either as representatives of their species or as isolated persons?

This question does present difficulties. Answering it is made easier if, as a kind of mental experiment, the way in which human aims and actions intertwine is demonstrated by means of a series of models. In this way, the inherently complex processes of interweaving are temporarily isolated in close focus, and thereby made more easily understandable. The models shortly to be described are, with the exception of the first, models of contests which (in the simpler forms at least) resemble real games like chess, bridge, football or tennis. They represent contests played out – more or less – according to rules. The first model, which we shall call the 'Primal Contest' is however a theoretically highly significant exception; it represents a real and deadly contest between two groups, and is not at all like a game. Both the Primal Contest and the game models are useful as an exercise in sociological imagination, which customary forms of thought tend to block. All the models are based on two or more people measuring their strength against each other. This is the basic situation encountered wherever people enter into or find themselves in relations with one another. The awareness of it, however, is often suppressed when people reflect on human relationships. There is no need to say why this is so. Every reader may think out the reasons for himself without much difficulty; he can look upon the task as a kind of game contest between himself and the author. In fact, challenges such as this are just what is under discussion here. They form a normal part of all human relationships. Smaller or larger trials of strength recur again and again: am I stronger? – are you stronger? After a while people may arrive at a certain balance of power, which according to social and personal circumstances may be stable or unstable.

For many people, the term 'power' has a rather unpleasant flavour. The reason is that during the whole development of human societies, power ratios have usually been extremely unequal; people or groups of people with relatively great power chances used to exercise those power chances to the full, often very brutally and unscrupulously for their own purposes. The offensive connotations which consequently cling to the concept 'power' may prevent people distinguishing between the factual data to which the concept of power refers and their evaluation of these data. So it is useful to concentrate here on the former. Balances of power are not only to be found in the great arena of relations between states, where they are often spectacular and attract most attention. They form an integral element of all human relationships. This is the way the following models should be read. It must also be borne in mind that power balances, like human relationships in general, are bi-polar at least, and usually multi-polar. The models may help towards a better understanding of such power balances, not as extraordinary but as everyday occurrences. From the day of his birth, a baby has power over its parents, not just the parents over the baby. At least, the baby has power over them as long as they attach any kind of value to it. If not, it loses its power. The parents may abandon the baby if it cries too much. They may starve it and, deliberately or not, cause it to die, if it has no function for them. Equally bi-polar is the balance of power between a slave and his master. The master has power over his slave, but the slave also has power over his master, in proportion to his function for his master – his master's dependence on him. In relationships between parents and infants, master and slave, power chances are distributed very unevenly. But whether the power differentials are large or small, balances of power are always present wherever there is functional interdependence between people. In this respect, simply to use the word 'power' is likely to mislead. We say that a person possesses great power, as if power were a thing he carried about in his pocket. This use of the word is a relic of magico-mythical ideas. Power is not an amulet possessed by one person and not by another; it is a structural characteristic of human relationships – of *all* human relationships.

The models demonstrate the relational character of power in a simplified form. In order to use the models of game contests to bring a series of power figurations into close focus, the concept of 'power ratios' is replaced here by the term 'relative strength of the players'. Even this phrase can be misunderstood as an absolute. However, it is obvious that a player's playing 'strength' varies in relation to his opponent's. The same goes for power, and for many other concepts in our language. The game models help to show how much clearer sociological problems become, and how much easier it is to deal with them if one reorganizes them in terms of balances rather than reifying terms. Concepts of balance are far more adequate for what can actually be observed in investigating the nexus of functions which interdependent human beings have for each other, than are concepts modelled on stationary objects.

Rule-governed human relationships cannot be understood if there is a tacit assumption that norms or rules are universally present from the outset as an unvarying property of human relationships. This assumption bars the way to asking and observing how and in what circumstances contests which are played out without rules transform themselves into relationships *with* set rules. Wars and other kinds of human relationships with few or no rules are proof enough that this is not merely a hypothetical problem. Sociological theories which make it appear that norms are the mainspring of social relationships cannot account for the possibility of human relationships without norms and regulations; they give a distorted view of human societies. This is why the game models are prefaced by the Primal Contest, a model which shows a relationship between two groups totally unregulated by norms. According to a strong sociological tradition, norms are identified with structure. The Primal Contest may serve as a reminder that it is perfectly possible for relationships between people to be structured even though they are played without rules. Even a situation that appears to be the height of disorder to the people involved in it forms part of a social order. There is no reason why historical 'disorders' – wars, revolutions, rebellions, massacres and power struggles of every kind – cannot be explained. To do that is in fact one of the tasks of sociology. It would be impossible to explain normless conflicts if they had no structure and, in that sense, no order. The distinction between 'order' and 'disorder', so significant for the people involved, is sociologically speaking without significance. *Among men, as in nature, no absolute chaos is possible.*

So, if the word 'society' is used here as a technical term for a specific level of integration, and if relationships at this level are seen as constituting an order of a particular kind, the word 'order' is not being used in the sense in which it is used when people speak of 'law and order' or, in adjectival form, of an 'orderly' as opposed to a 'disorderly' person. One is talking about an order in the same sense that one talks of a natural order, in which decay and destruction as structured processes have their place alongside growth and synthesis, death and disintegration alongside birth and integration. For the people involved, these manifestations seem, with good cause, to be contradictory and irreconcilable. As objects of *study,* they are indivisible and of equal importance. Therefore it would be misleading to explain the process of social interweaving only in terms of models which refer to human relationships regulated by fixed norms. The Primal Contest may serve as a reminder of what it *is* that becomes socially regulated.

Primal Contest: model of a contest without rules

Two small tribal groups, A and B, get in each other's way when hunting for food in a great tract of wild forest. Both are hungry. For reasons not apparent to either, it has for some time been getting more and more difficult for them to find enough to eat. Game has become scarcer, roots and wild fruit harder to find, and the rivalry and enmity between the two groups has grown consequently fiercer. Group A consists of big powerfully-built men and women, with few young people or children. Group B, their opponents, are smaller, less powerfully-built, quicker on their feet and, on average, considerably younger.

So the two groups get in each other's way. They are caught up in a long drawn-out struggle with each other. The smaller people of Group B creep at night into the other's camp, kill one or two of them in the dark, and vanish swiftly when the dead men's fellows, slower and more heavily built, try to pursue them. The men of Group A have their revenge some time later. They kill women and children of Group B while the men are out hunting.

Here, as in other similar cases, a fairly enduring antagonism reveals itself as a form of functional interdependence. The two groups are rivals for shrinking food resources. They are dependent upon each other: as in a game of chess (which was originally a war game), each move of one group determines each move of the other group and *vice versa*. The internal arrangements in each group are determined to a greater or lesser extent by what each group thinks the other might do next. Fierce antagonists, in other words, perform a function for each other, because the interdependence of human beings due to their hostility is no less a functional relationship than that due to their position as friends, allies, and specialists bonded to each other through the division of labour. Their function for each other is in the last resort based on the compulsion they exert over each other by reason of their interdependence. It is not possible to explain the actions, plans and aims of either of the two groups if they are conceptualized as the freely chosen decisions, plans and aims of each group considered on its own, independently of the other group. They can be explained only if one takes into account the compelling forces the groups exert upon each other by reason of their interdependence, their bilateral function for each other as enemies.

The concept of 'function', as it has been used in some sociological and anthropological literature, especially by 'structural-functionalist' theorists, is not only based on an inadequate analysis of the subject matter to which it relates, but also contains an inappropriate value judgement which, moreover, is made explicit in neither interpretation nor use. The inappropriateness of the evaluation is due to the fact that they tend – unintentionally – to use the terms for those tasks performed by one part of the society which are 'good' for the 'whole', because they contribute to the preservation and integrity of the existing social system. Human activities which either fail or appear to fail to do that are therefore branded as 'dysfunctional'. It is plain that at this point social beliefs have become mixed up in scientific theory. For this reason alone it is useful to look more carefully into the implications of the model of the two warring tribal groups. As enemies they perform a function for each other of which one must be aware if one is to understand the actions and plans of either of the two tribal groups. Here, as can be seen, the term 'function' is not used as an expression for a task performed by a section within a harmonious 'whole'. The model indicates that, like the concept of power, the concept of function must be understood as a concept of *relationship*. We can only speak of social functions when referring to interdependencies which constrain people to a greater or lesser extent. This element of coercion can be clearly seen in the function performed by each tribal group as the enemy of the other. The difficulty in using the concept of function as a quality of a single social unit is simply that it leaves out the reciprocity, the bi-polarity or multi-polarity of all functions. It is impossible to understand the function A performs for B without talking into account the function B performs for A. That is what is meant when it is said that the concept of function is a concept of relationship.

To put it at its simplest, one could say: when one person (or a group of persons) lacks something which another person or group has the power to withhold, the latter has a function for the former. Thus men have a function for women and women for men, parents for children and children for parents. Enemies have a function for each other, because once they have become interdependent they have the power to withhold from each other such elementary requirements as that of preserving their physical and social integrity, and ultimately of survival.

To understand the concept of 'function' in this way demonstrates its connection with power within human relationships. People or groups which have functions for each other exercise constraint over each other. Their potential for withholding from each other what they require is usually uneven, which means that the constraining power of one side is greater than that of the other. Changes in the structure of societies, in the overall nexus of functional interdependencies, may induce one group to question another group's power of constraint, their 'potential for withholding'. In that case, these changes initiate trials of strength, which can erupt suddenly in the form of acute and even violent power struggles, or they may smoulder for long periods of time as a standing conflict inherent in the structure of a society during a certain phase of its development. Today, built-in tensions and conflicts of this kind are characteristic of the interdependent functions of workers and entrepreneurs, as of those between groups of states. In previous periods, they were characteristic of the triangular relationship between kings, nobles and citizens, or between segments of a tribe.[3] They are no less characteristic of the functional interdependencies between husbands and wives or parents and children. At the root of these trials of strength are usually problems such as these: Whose potential for withholding what the other requires is greater? Who, accordingly, is more or less dependent on the other? Who, therefore, has to submit or adapt himself more to the other's demands? In more general terms, who has the higher power ratio, and can therefore steer the activities of the other side to a greater extent than they can steer his own activities – can put more pressure on them than they can put on him? If the overall structure of societies changes, the question may become whether one side can defunctionalize the other, destroy the whole set of social positions on which the other side's power rests, or physically destroy its opponents altogether.[4]

The Primal Contest represents as it were a borderline case. Here, one side aims at depriving the other not only of their social functions but of their very lives. In studying men's changing interdependencies and the interweaving of their aims and activities, one cannot lose sight of the interdependence of violent antagonists represented by the Primal Contest model. Only if one is aware of this last resort relationship between humans – interdependence through an all-out struggle for survival – is it possible to see the basic nature of the problems mentioned before: how have people been able – and how are they able – to regulate some of their interdependencies in such a way that they need not resort to this ultimate way out of tensions and conflicts? At the same time, this model of a contest without rules can serve as a reminder that all relationships between men, all their functional interdependencies, are processes. Today these concepts are often used in a manner which suggests that they refer to a stationary condition, in which any change is quite accidental. Terms like 'interweaving' point to the processual nature of such relationships.

Returning to the example of the course of the struggle between two tribes, it shows clearly the immanent dynamics of a conflict relationship. In such a life-or-death conflict, each side is constantly both planning its next foray and living always on the alert in anticipation of the other side's next move. Since they have no common norms as a means of orientation, each side relies for its orientation entirely on its idea of the power resources of the other side in relation to its own – on its idea of their respective strength, cunning, weapons, food supply and food reserves. These power resources and relative strength, which in this case means above all physical force and the planning of strategies for physical survival and annihilation, is constantly being tested in raids and skirmishes. Each side tries to weaken the other by any means. Here one is indeed confronted with a continuous inter-weaving, more upon move, in which every single person is totally involved. In this case, as can be seen, groups are no longer represented in terms of concepts such as norms, rules, ideal-types and so on, which make it appear that they are constituted exclusively through intellectual processes; the interweaving concerns human beings in the round. The models have to be read as representations of human beings bonded to each other in time and space. Among the problems implied by the Primal Contest model are the following: Will the group of older, taller, more muscular but slower people succeed in enticing the nimbler, smaller, less experienced but more agile people away from their camp and kill some of their women and children? Will the latter group succeed in goading the first with abuse until they become furious and pursue the second group, stumble into their traps and get killed? Will they weaken and destroy each other to the point where both are beyond recovery? That is why even this case of the interdependence between violent enemies locked in a life-and-death struggle is a *process* of interweaving. The sequence of moves on either side can only be understood and explained in terms of the immanent dynamics of their interdependence. If the sequence of actions of either side were studied in isolation, it would appear without rhyme or reason. The functional interdependence of the moves of the two sides is no less great in this case than in the case of rule-governed conflict or cooperation. Even though the interweaving of the two sides in the sequence of time is a process without norms, it is nevertheless a process with a clear structure which can be analysed and explained.

Game models: models of interweaving processes with norms

Like the opening model of a contest without rules, the models of game contests with rules are simplifying intellectual experiments. With their help it is possible to bring out more graphically the processual character of relationships between interdependent people. At the same time, they show how the web of human relations changes when the distribution of power changes. One of the ways in which simplification has been brought about is by substituting a series of assumptions about players' relative strength in the game for differences in relative power potentials of interdependent people or groups in their relations with each other. The models are arranged in such a way as to bring out more clearly the transformation which the web of human inter-relations undergoes when power differentials decrease.

Two-person games

(1a) Imagine a game played by two people, in which one player is very much superior to the other, A being a very strong player, B a very weak one. In this case, A has a very high measure of control over B. To a certain extent A can force B to make particular moves. In other words, A has 'power' over B. This term means no more and no less than that A can control B's moves to a very great extent. But this 'capacity to compel' is not unlimited; player B, relatively weak though he is, has a degree of power over A. For just as B, in making each move, has to take his bearings from A's preceding moves, so must A take his bearing's from B's preceding moves. B may not be as strong as A, but he must have some strength – if it were zero, there would be no game. In other words, in any game the participants always have control *over each other*. When speaking of the 'power' A has over B, the concept does not refer to an absolute, but to a *power ratio* – the difference (in A's favour) between A's and B's strength in the game. This difference – the uneven balance between the two players' strengths in the game – determines to what extent player A's moves can shape player B's moves, or *vice versa*. According to the assumptions of model (1a), the differential between the players' strengths in the game (their power ratio) in A's favour is very great. Correspondingly great is A's ability to force a particular move (a particular 'behaviour' or 'action') on his opponent.[5]

However, A's greater strength in the game does not only give him a high degree of control over his opponent B. It also gives him, *in addition,* a high degree of control over the game as such. Though his control of the game is not absolute, he can determine its course (the game process) and therefore also the result of the game, to a very great extent. In interpreting this model, it is important to make this conceptual distinction between two kinds of control which result from one player's greatly superior strength: on the one hand, the control he can exert over his opponent, and, on the other hand, the control it gives him over the course of the game as such. That is not to say that because it is possible to make this distinction between control over the player and control over the game, that one can think and speak as if the player and the game exist independently of each other.

(1b)   Imagine that the differential between A's strength and B's strength in the game diminishes. It does not matter whether this comes about by B's strength increasing or by A's decreasing. A's chances of controlling B's moves by means of his own – that is, his power over B – diminishes proportionately; B's chances of controlling A increase correspondingly. The same is true of A's ability to determine the game process and result. The more the differential between A's and B's strength decreases, the less power will either player have to force a particular tactic on the other. Both players will have correspondingly less chance to control the changing figuration of the game; and the less dependent will be the changing figuration of the game on the aims and plans for the course of the game which each player has formed by himself. The stronger, conversely, becomes the dependence of each of the two players' overall plans and of each of their moves on the changing figuration of the game – on the game process. The more the game comes to resemble a social process, the less it comes to resemble the implementation of an individual plan. In other words, to the extent that the inequality in the strengths of the two players diminishes, there will result from the interweaving of moves of two individual people a game process *which neither of them has planned.*

Multi-person games at one level

(2a)   Imagine a game in which player A is playing simultaneously against several other players, B, C, D and so on, under the following conditions: A is far superior in strength to any single one of his opponents, and he is playing against each one separately. In this case the figuration of the players is not very different from that in model 1a. Players B, C, D and so on are not playing jointly but separately, and the only connection between them therefore is the fact that each individual is playing privately against the same equally superior opponent, A. It is therefore basically a series of games for two people, each game having its own balance of power and developing in its own way. The courses taken by the games are not directly interdependent. In each of these games A is overwhelmingly the more powerful; he has a very high degree of control both over his opponent and over the course of the game itself. In each of these games the distribution of power is unequivocally unequal, inelastic and stable. Perhaps one ought to add that the position might alter to A's disadvantage, if the number of independent games he is playing should increase. It is possible that his superiority in strength over the independent players, B, C, D and the rest, might gradually suffer as a result of an increase in the number of opponents, all independent of each other. There is a limit to the span of active relationships independent one from another which one person can pursue simultaneously – in separate compartments, so to speak.

(2b) Imagine a game in which player A plays simultaneously against several weaker opponents, not separately but against all of them together. Thus he plays a single game against a group of opponents, each one of whom taken by himself is weaker than A.

This model allows for various constellations in the balance of power. The simplest is that in which players B, C, D and their colleagues form a group directed against A, and are undisturbed by tensions among themselves. Even in this case there is more doubt than in (2a) about the distribution of power between A and the opposing group, and about the possibility of one side or the other controlling the course of the game. Undoubtedly the unequivocal formation of a group by many weaker players represents a lessening of A's superiority. Compared with (1a) there is much less certainty about the control and planning of the game and therefore less certainty in predicting its outcome. If groups formed by weaker players do not have strong inner tensions, that is a power factor to their advantage. Conversely, if groups formed by weaker players do have strong inner tensions, that is a power factor to the advantage of their opponent. The greater the tensions, the greater the chances of A to control the moves of B, C, D and their allies, as well as the general course of the game.

In contrast with models of type (1) and the transitional model

(2a) in which the games in question are for two people, or, to put it differently, bi-polar groups, (2b) is an example of a multi-polar game or a game for several people. It can be regarded as a transitional model to (2c).

(2c)   Imagine that A's strength decreases in a multi-polar game, compared with that of his opponents, B, C, D and others. A's chances to control the moves of his opponents, and to control the course of the game as such, change in the same direction as in (1b), provided that the group of opponents is fairly united.

(2d)   Imagine a game in which two groups, B, C, D, E, . . . and U, V, W, X, . . . play against each other according to rules which give both sides equal chances of winning, and with each side having approximately the same strength. In this case neither side is able to exercise a decisive influence over the other in the flurry of move and countermove. The game process in this case cannot be controlled by either of the two groups on its own. The intertwining of moves made alternately by each player and group of players builds up to form a certain kind of order, which can be defined and explained. But, in order to do so, an observer needs to distance himself from the positions taken by both sides, as they appear when considered alone. The order in question is a specific kind of order, an ordered network or figuration, within which no action by either side can be regarded as the action of that one side alone. It must rather be interpreted as continuing the inter-weaving process and forming a part of the future interweaving of actions made by both sides.

Multi-person games on several levels

Imagine a game for many people, in which the number of partici-pants is constantly growing. This increases the pressure on the players to change their grouping and organization. An individual player will have to wait longer and longer for his turn to move. It will become more and more difficult for a player to put together a mental picture of the course of the game and its figuration. Lacking such a picture, he may become disorientated. He needs a fairly clear picture of the course of the game and of its general figuration, which changes constantly as the game pro-ceeds, so that he may plan his next move accordingly. The figura-tion of interdependent players and of the game which they play together is the framework for each individual's moves. He must be in a position to picture this figuration so that he may decide which move will give him the best chance of winning or of defending himself against his opponents' attacks. But there is a limit to the span of the web of interdependence within which an individual player can orientate himself suitably and plan his personal strategy over a series of moves. If the number of interdependent players grows, the figuration, development and direction of the game will become more and more opaque to the individual player. However strong he may be, he will become less and less able to control them. From the point of view of the individual player, therefore, an intertwining network of more and more players functions increasingly as though it had a life of its own. Here too the game is nothing more than a game played by many individuals. But as the number of players grows the individual player not only finds the game increasingly opaque and uncontrollable, but he also gradually becomes *aware* of his inability to understand and control it. Both the figuration of the game and the individual player's picture of it – the way in which he perceives the course of the game – change together in a specific direction. They change in functional interdependence, as two inseparable dimensions of the same process. They can be considered separately, but not as *being* separate.

As the number of players grows, it becomes harder for each individual – and therefore for all the players – to make suitable or correct moves, judged from his own position in the totality of the game. The game will become increasingly disorganized; its functioning will deteriorate. As functioning deteriorates,[6] a growing pressure is exerted on the group of players to reorganize themselves. There are several possibilities open; three will be mentioned here, though it is possible to examine only one of them at length.

An increase in the number of players can cause the group of players to distintegrate, splintering into a number of smaller groups. Their relationship to each other can take two possible forms. The splinter groups can either move further apart and then continue to play the game quite independently of every other group. Or they can make up a new figuration of interdependent groups, each playing more or less autonomously, though all remain rivals for certain chances, equally sought after by all groups. A third possibility is that the group of players – in certain circumstances which cannot be entered into here – remains integrated, turning, however into a highly complex figuration; a two-tier group can develop out of the one-tier group.

(3a)   *Two-tier games model: oligarchic type*

Pressure exerted on the individual players by an increase in the number of players can cause a change within the group of players. From a group in which every individual plays together on the same level it may turn into a 'two-level' or 'two-tier' group of players. All players remain interdependent, but they no longer all play directly with each other. This function is taken over by the special functionaries who coordinate the game – representatives, delegates, leaders, governments, royal courts, monopolistic élites and so forth. Together they form a second, smaller group, a second-tier group as one might say. These are the people who play directly with and against each other, but they are nevertheless bound in one way or another to the mass of players who now make up the first storey. Also, there can be no second level without a first level; the people on the second level have no function except with regard to those on the first level. Both levels are dependent on each other and possess different reciprocal power chances corresponding to the degree of their dependence on each other. But the distribution of power between the people of the first and second levels can vary enormously. The power differential between the players of the first and second tier can be very great – in the latter's favour – and it can become smaller and smaller.

Let us take the first case. The power differential between first and second tier is very large. Only the players of the second tier participate directly and actively in the game. They have a monopoly over access to the game: every player in the second level finds himself in a circle of activity, such as can already be observed in single-level games. There is a small number of players, so every player is in a position to picture the figuration of players and game; he can plan his strategy in accordance with this picture and intervene directly with each move in the perpetually moving figuration of the game. In addition he can influence this figuration to a greater or lesser extent, depending on his own position within the group, and he can follow the consequences of his moves for the progress of the game. He can observe other players' counter-moves, and how the interweaving of his own moves with those of others is expressed through the constantly changing figuration of the game. He may imagine that the course of the game, as he sees it unfold before him, is more or less transparent to him. Members of pre-industrial oligarchic élites – for example courtiers, men like the duc de Saint-Simon, memoir-writer in the time of Louis XIV – usually felt that they had a precise knowledge of the unwritten rules governing the game at the hub of the state-society.

The illusion that the game is essentially transparent is never completely justified in reality; and two-tier figurations – not to mention three-, four- and five-tier figurations, which are left out here for the sake of simplicity – are far too complicated constructions for their structure and direction of development to be clarified without thorough scientific investigation. But such investigations only begin to be possible at a stage of development where people are able at the same time to be aware of their lack of knowledge. This enables them to recognize the relative opacity of the game to which their moves relate, and the possibility of amending their lack of knowledge by means of systematic research. This is only marginally possible within the framework of dynastic aristocratic societies which correspond to an oligarchic two-tier model. The game played by the group on the upper level will be viewed by the players not as a game process but as an an accumulation of actions of individuals. The explanatory value of this 'view of the game' is the more limited because no individual player in a two-tier game, however great his strength, has anything like the same ability as player A in model (1a) to control the other players or, more important, to determine the game process. Even in a game with no more than two tiers, the figuration of game and players already possesses a degree of complexity which prevents any one individual from using his superiority to guide the game in the direction of his own goals and wishes. He makes his moves both *out of* the network and *into* the network of interdependent players where there are alliances and enmities, cooperation and rivalry at different levels. At least three, if not four, different balances of power may be distinguished in a two-tier game. They interlock like cogwheels, and so people who are enemies on one level may be allies on another. First there is the power balance within the small group at the upper level, secondly the power balance between players at the first level and players at the second, thirdly the power balance between the groups at the lower level and, if one wishes to go even further, one might add the power balance *within* each of these lower-level groups.

Models with three, four, five and more levels would have power balances which were correspondingly more interwoven. In fact they would be better, more suitable models for the majority of contemporary state-societies.[7] We will limit ourselves here to two-tier games models.

In a two-tier game of the older, oligarchic kind, the balance of power in favour of the upper tier is very disproportionate, inelastic and stable. The smaller circle of players on the upper level is very superior in strength to the larger circle on the lower level. Nevertheless, the interdependence of the two circles imposes limitations on every player, even on those at the upper level. Even a player on the upper level in a position of very great strength has less scope for controlling the course of the game than, for example, player A in model (2b). Also, it is remarkable how much slighter are his scope for control and his chances of controlling the game than those of player A in model (1a). There is a good reason for stressing this difference again: in historical descriptions – which are often concerned only with the small circle of players on the higher levels of a multi-level society – the actions of the players in question are quite often explained as if they were the moves of player A in model (1a). But in reality the three or four interdependent balances of power in a two-tier oligarchic model make possible many constellations which considerably limit the chances for control of even the stronger player on the upper level. If the overall balance of such a game allows for the possibility that all players on both levels may unite and play together against the strongest player, A, then A's chance of using strategy to force them to make the moves which seem desirable to him are extremely slight, and their chance of using strategy to force him to make the moves they have chosen is very good. On the other hand if there are rival groups of players on the upper level, which are fairly equal in strength and balance each other out, without one or other of them holding the key to decisive victory, then an individual player A, on the higher level but standing outside any of the groupings, will have a good chance of guiding the rival groups and thereby the course of the game, as long as he does it with the greatest caution and the greatest understanding of the characteristics of these complex figurations. In this case his strength rests on the insight and skill with which he can seize the chances offered by the constellation of power weightings, and make them the basis of his strategy. In the absence of A, the groups on the lower levels will be strengthened by rivalry between groups on the upper level.

(3b) *Game models on two levels: simplified increasingly democratic type*

Imagine a two-level model in which the strength of the lower-level players is growing slowly but steadily in relation to the strength of the upper-level players. If power differentials between the two groups diminish, reducing their inequality, then the balance of power will become more flexible and elastic. It will be more likely to fluctuate, in one direction or the other.

A, the strongest player on the upper level, may still be superior to the other upper-level players. When the lower-level players become more powerful, moves made by A during the game will fall under the sway of a far more complicated figuration than that influencing A in the previous model (3a). There too the grouping of the players who form the lower tier has no mean bearing on the course of the game. But it still has comparatively little manifest power, and as good as no direct sway on the grouping of the upper level. Usually the lower-level players exercise only latent and indirect influence, one reason for which is that they lack organization. Among the manifest signs of their latent strength are the never-ending vigilance of the upper-level players and the closely-woven net of precautions serving to keep them under control, and which is often tightened when their potential strength increases. In any case the dependencies which bind the upper-level players to those of the lower level constrain the former much less noticeably. Their superiority is still so vast that they are often inclined to the conviction that they are absolutely free of the low-level players and can conduct themselves in whatever way they like. They feel themselves to be constrained and confined only by their interdependence with their fellow-players on the same level, and by the balance of power existing between them.

If power differentials between the two levels decrease, the dependencies which bind the upper to the lower level will become stronger – and since they are stronger, all the participants will become more aware of them. They will become more noticeable. If power differentials diminish further, the functions of upper-level players change and in the end the players themselves change. As long as power differentials are great, it will appear to people on the upper level as if the whole game and the lower-level players in particular are there for their benefit. As power balances shift, this state of affairs changes. Increasingly it appears to all participants as though the upper-level players are there for the benefit of the lower-level players. The former gradually become more openly and unambiguously functionaries, spokesmen or representatives of one or other of the lower-level groups. In model (3a) the game within the small upper-level circle is clearly the centre of the whole two-tier game, and the lower-level players appear on the whole to be peripheral figures, mere statistics. But in model (3b), as the influence of the lower-level players over the game grows, the game becomes increasingly complex for all players on the upper level. Each one's strategy, in his relations with the lower-level groups he represents, becomes as important an aspect of the game as his strategy in relation to the other upper-level players. Every individual player is now constrained and confined to a much greater degree, kept in check by the number of simultaneous interdependent games he must play with players or groups of players who are becoming less and less socially inferior. The overall figuration of these interwoven games becomes visibly differentiated and often cannot be clearly surveyed even by the most gifted player, so that it becomes more and more difficult for a player to decide entirely on his own which will be the most suitable next move.

Upper-level players – party oligarchs, for example – are increasingly able to be effective in their special positions only if they become members of more or less organized groups. Groups of players from *both* levels may indeed still band together to form a kind of figuration which enables an individual to maintain a balance between interdependent but rival groups. In this way he reaches a position which gives him greater power chances than any other individual in the figuration. But under conditions which bring about a decrease in power differentials – a general diffusion of power chances among players and groups of players – if a figuration makes unusually great power chances accessible to a single player or small group of players, it will be extremely unstable, in accordance with this latent power structure. Such a figuration will usually only emerge in times of crisis and can only with considerable difficulty be maintained for a longer period. Even a player presently in a position of particular strength will now be far more answerable to players on the lower level whose position has become stronger, than was a player in a similarly strong position under the conditions prevailing in model (3a). The game puts a constant strain on a player in this position, a much greater strain than on a similarly placed player under the conditions of model (3a). Under conditions like those in model (3a), a player and his group in such a position may in fact appear to control and guide the whole game themselves. As the distribution of power weightings becomes less unequal and more diffuse, it also becomes plainer how little the game can be controlled and guided from any single player's or group's position. Indeed, the opposite is the case. It becomes clear how much the course of the game – which is the product of the interweaving moves of a large number of players, between whom there is a diminished and diminishing power differential – determines in its turn the structure of the moves of every single player.

The conception players have of their game will change accordingly – that is their 'ideas', the means of speech and thought by which they attempt to assimilate and master their experience of the game. Instead of players believing that the game takes its shape from the individual moves of individual people, there is a slowly growing tendency for impersonal concepts to be developed to master their experience of the game. These impersonal concepts take into account the relative autonomy of the game process from the intentions of individual players. A long and laborious process is involved, working out communicable means of thought which will correspond to the character of the game as something not immediately controllable, even by the players themselves. Metaphors are used which oscillate constantly between the idea that the course of the game can be reduced to the actions of individual players and the other idea that it is of a supra-personal nature. Because the game cannot be controlled by the players, it is easily perceived as a kind of 'superhuman' entity. For a long time it is especially difficult for players to comprehend that their inability to control the game derives from their mutual dependence and positioning as players, and from the tensions and conflicts inherent in this intertwining network.

Commentary

1. Whatever their theoretical content, these models of interweaving are not theoretical in the customary sense of the word. They are

didactic models. Their primary purpose here is to facilitate a reorientation of our powers of imagination and conceptualization in order to understand the nature of the tasks confronting sociology. People say that the task of sociology is to investigate society. But it is not made at all clear what we are to understand by 'society'. In many ways sociology seems to be a science in search of a subject. This is partly because the verbal materials and conceptual tools our language puts at our disposal for defining and investigating this subject are not flexible enough. Any attempt to develop them further so that they correspond to the peculiarity of this subject matter will cause difficulties in communication. These didactic models are a means of overcoming such difficulties. By using the image of people playing a game as a metaphor for people forming societies together, it is easier to rethink the static ideas which are associated with most of the current concepts used in this context. They must be transformed into the far more versatile concepts which are needed if we are to improve our mental equipment for tackling the problems of sociology. One only needs to compare the imaginative possibilities of such static concepts as the individual and society or ego and system with the imaginative possibilities opened up by the metaphoric use of various images of games and players; the comparison will help us to understand that these models have served to unleash our powers of imagination.

2. At the same time the models serve to make certain problems about social life more accessible to scientific reflection. These problems actually play a central part in all human relationships, but are too often ignored in theorizing about them. The most important of them is the *problem of power.* In part its neglect can be traced back to the simple fact that the social phenomena to which this concept refers are extremely complex. To simplify the problem, a single form – perhaps the military or the economic form – of the many possible sources of power which can be accessible to people is often taken as *the* source of power, to which all forms of the exercise of power may be traced. But this simply conceals the problem. The difficulties encountered in reflecting on problems of power stem from the polymorphous nature of sources of power. To explore the problems raised here either at length or exclusively is not the purpose of these models. The task here is not to solve the problem of power but simply to bring it in out of the cold and make it easily accessible as one

of the central problems of sociological effort. The necessity for doing this is connected with the obvious difficulty of examining questions of power without becoming emotionally involved. Another person's power is to be feared: he can compel us to do a particular thing whether we want to or not. Power is suspect: people use their power to exploit others for their own ends. Power seems unethical: everyone ought to be in a position to make all his own decisions. And the mist of fear and suspicion which clings to this concept is understandably transferred to its use in a scientific theory. One may say that someone 'has' power and leave it at that, although such usage, which implies that power is a thing, leads down a blind alley. A more adequate solution to problems of power depends on power being understood unequivocally as a structural characteristic of a relationship, all-pervading and, as a structural characteristic, neither good nor bad. It may be both. We depend on others; others depend on us. In so far as we are more dependent on others than they are on us, more directed by others than they are by us, they have power over us, whether we have become dependent on them by their use of naked force or by our need to be loved, our need for money, healing, status, a career, or simply for excitement. Be that as it may, in direct relationships between two people, A's relationship to B is also always B's relationship to A. In such relationships A's dependence on B is always connected with B's dependence on A, except in marginal situations. But it is possible for one to be very much slighter than the other. It may be the case that B's power over A, his chance of controlling and guiding A's course of action, is greater than A's power over B. This balance of power is weighted in B's favour. The models in the first series illustrate some of the simplest types of balance of power in direct relationships between two people, and the corresponding outcomes of the relationships. At the same time they may also help to correct our habit of using the concept of relationship as a static concept, and to remind us that all relationships – like human games – are processes.

But relationships, and the conditions of dependence involved in them, may comprise not just two but many people. Take a figuration formed by many interdependent people, in which all positions are endowed with approximately equal power chances. A is not more powerful than B, nor B more powerful than C, nor C more powerful than D and so on, and *vice versa*. Being interdependent with so many people will very probably often compel individual people to act in a way they would not act except under compulsion. In this case one is inclined to personify or reify interdependence. The mythology dictated by linguistic usage urges us to believe that there must be 'someone' who 'has power'. So, because we feel the pressure of 'power', we always invent a person who exercises it, or a kind of superhuman entity like 'nature 'or 'society' in which we say power resides. In thought, we hold them responsible for the constraints to which we feel ourselves subject. There are certain practical and theoretical disadvantages in our not at the moment being able to distinguish clearly between the constraints which *every possible inter-dependence* between people exerts over those people – even in a figuration where all positions are equally endowed with power chances – and the constraints which stem from the variation in power chances between different social positions. But we cannot now go into the range of problems glimpsed here. It must suffice to say that the potential people we are born would never develop into the actual people we become if we were never subjected to any of the constraints of interdependence. But that is most certainly not to say that present forms of interdependence exercise the kind of constraint which is conducive to optimal realization of human potentials.

3. In model (1a) the structure of the game is largely determined by the intentions and actions of *one* person. The course of the game can be explained in terms of the plans and goals of one individual. Thus model (1a) probably corresponds best with the ideas of a large number of people about how social events can be explained. At the same time it is reminiscent of a well-known theoretical model of society, which starts with the interaction of two individuals who were independent of each other to begin with. Expressed differently, it starts with the interaction of 'ego' and 'alter'. But the model has not been properly thought through. The relationship is still fundamentally seen as a state, not a process. The problems raised by this view of the nature of human inter-dependencies and power balances, together with all related problems, are still beyond the horizons of so-called action theories. At most they take into account the fact that intentional inter-actions have unintended consequences. But they conceal a cir-cumstance which is central to sociological theory and practice, namely that unintentional human interdependencies lie at the

root of every intentional interaction. The Primal Contest model perhaps expresses this most directly. It is not possible to construct an adequate sociological model without taking into consideration that there are types of interdependence which impel ego and alter to fight and kill each other.

As a model for certain relationships, model (1a) is certainly of use. There are cases to which it can be applied, and it would be a mistake to disregard it. The relationship between player A and player B may be similar to that between a specialist and a non-specialist, a slave-owner and a slave, or a famous painter and a patron. As a model of societies, however, model (1a) is at best of marginal use.

By contrast, model (2c), and model (3b) even more, offer a certain amount of help towards understanding what we mentioned as the basic experience of the nascent science of sociology — the experience that out of the intertwining of many people's actions there may emerge social consequences which no one has planned. Both these game models indicate the conditions under which players may slowly begin to encounter a problem: that a game process, which comes about entirely as a result of the interweaving of the individual moves of many players, takes a course *which none of the individual players has planned, determined or anticipated.* On the contrary, the unplanned course of the game repeatedly influences the moves of each individual player. So these models help to shed some light on one of the main problems facing sociology, insufficient understanding of which constantly leads to misunderstandings about the subject matter and problems of sociology.

There is constant discussion about what the subject matter of sociology actually is. If the answer is 'society', as is often claimed, then many will think of it as an aggregation of individual people. The question one encounters most often runs like this: Can anything be said about society which could not be found out from studying individual people, for example, from physiological or individual psychological analyses? Model (2c) and in particular, model (3b) show us in which direction we must seek the answers to such questions. These models point to the possibility that the course of a game played by 30, 300 or 3000 players cannot be controlled and guided by any of those players. As the gap between the power potentials of the players decreases, this becomes the more probable. Here the game process gains relative autonomy from the plans and intentions of any of the individual players who create and maintain the game by their actions. This can be expressed negatively by saying that the course of the game is not in the power of any one player. The other side of the coin is that the course of the game itself has power over the behaviour and thought of the individual players. For their actions and ideas cannot be explained and understood if they are considered on their own; they need to be understood and explained within the framework of the game. The model shows how people's interdependence as players exerts constraint over each of the individuals bonded together in this way; the constraint stems from the particular nature of their relatedness and interdependence as players. In this instance, too, power is the structural characteristic of a relationship. On first meeting models of type (3b), it may seem puzzling that we can no longer point to any one individual or even any single group of individuals who exercise unilateral power over all the others. After a while it becomes easier to understand that as power differentials lessen between interdependent individuals and groups there is a diminishing possibility that any participants, whether on their own or as groups, will be able to influence the overall course of the game. But chances to control the game may increase again as people become more and more distanced from their own intertwining network, and gain more insight into the structure and dynamics of the game. The relative autonomy of sociology in relation to disciplines like physiology and psychology which concern themselves with individual people, is ultimately based on the relative autonomy in relation to individual actions, of the structural processes which result from the interdependence and interweaving of the actions of many people. This autonomy always exists, but people become especially sharply conscious of it at times when society is becoming increasingly differentiated, and chains of interdependence are lengthening. The increasing number of individuals forming these chains are bound together across increasing distances by the specialization of their functions. Given the conditions of this figuration, it is especially noticeable that the processes of interweaving are self-regulating, and relatively autonomous in relation to the people who form the web. In sum, we are dealing with a level of integration which, in relation to lower levels of integration like individual human organisms, evinces specific characteristics, forms of organization which are quite inaccessible to comprehension and scientific investigation if we attempt to explain them solely by reducing them to their individual components (individual people, individual organisms) as in psychological or biological forms of explanation.

Game models are an excellent way of representing the distinctiveness of the forms of organization which are met with on the level of integration represented by human societies. Our heritage of speech and thought puts a certain pressure on us to interpret all nexuses of events as unilinear chains of cause and effect. Two explanations of unilinear chains are closely related. The older is in terms of the actions of a personal Creator. Gradually during the course of human history, this explanation has been joined by the unilinear chain explanation in terms of an impersonal cause. When complex patterns of interweaving are encountered, it is usual to try to explain even these in terms of the same categories of cause and effect and the same picture of unilinear sequences. Only, in this case, people usually imagine that all that is necessary is to make a big bundle of short, unilinear, connecting chains of this sort. Instead of explaining whatever needs to be explained in terms of a cause or a Creator, they explain it by means of five, ten or even a hundred 'factors', 'variables' or whatever the term may be. But just try to apply this type of explanation to a player's twelfth move in a two-person game on one level, where both players are equally strong. We are inclined to interpret this move in terms of the character of the person who made it. Perhaps it might be explained psychologically as a manifestation of his great intelligence or, more physiologically, in terms of his overtiredness. Any of these explanations might be justifiable but none of them is sufficient. For the twelfth move in such a game can no longer be adequately explained in terms of short, unilinear causal sequences. Nor can an explanation be based on the individual character of one or other player. This move can only be interpreted in the light of the way the preceding moves of both players have intertwined, and of the specific figuration which has resulted from this intertwining. Any attempt to ascribe this intertwining to one or other player alone, or even to a mere accumulation of both as originator or cause, is doomed to inadequacy. Only the progressive interweaving of moves during the game process, and its result – the figuration of the game prior to the twelfth move – can be of service in explaining the twelfth move. The player uses this figuration to orientate himself before making his move. Yet this process of interweaving

D

and the current state or figuration of the game, by which the individual player orientates himself, exhibit an order of their own. That order is a phenomenon with structures, connections and regularities of distinctive kinds, none of which exists above and beyond individuals, but is rather the result of the continual combination and interweaving of individuals. All we say about 'societies' or 'social facts' refers to this order which, as we have said, includes specific types of 'disorder' resembling those in the Primal Contest model, as well as constantly recurring types of disintegrative or unravelling processes.

When we consider this, it becomes obvious that many of the customary conceptual structures, which force themselves on our attempts to think about such facts, do not correspond to the particular level of integration to which they refer. Among them, for example, are much-used turns of phrase like 'man and his environment' or his 'social background'. Consider game models. It would not occur to anyone to describe the game process in which a player cooperates with and against others, as his 'environment', 'surroundings' or 'background'. The contrast which is repeatedly drawn between 'individual' and 'society' makes it seem as though individuals could in some sense exist independently of society, and *vice versa*. This seems highly questionable in the light of models showing processes of interweaving. And it is a scientific superstition that in order to investigate them scientifically one must necessarily dissect processes of interweaving into their component parts. Sociologists often no longer do this, although a number of them seem to have guilty consciences about their omission.

Sociologists, especially when they are working empirically, often use a theoretical framework and conceptual tools which are mostly quite well suited to the distinctive character of the particular kind of order produced by human interweaving, and to the character of societies and changing figurations made up of interdependent people. But there is perhaps still a need for them to work out clearly what they are doing, to become fully aware of it, and so to justify it. Consider for example Durkheim's explanation of certain regularities in suicide rates for various groups of people. He bases it on specific differences between the interweaving-structures they belong to. Statistics play an essential part; but their function is that of indicators, pointing to specific variations in the way people are caught up in a network of relationships. Whether one is trying to study the relationships between kings and parliaments in medieval Europe[8] or whether one is investigating the relationship between 'the established and the outsiders'[9] or the strategy of a charismatic leader or of an absolute ruler in the inner circles of his court, one is always dealing with interweaving of the kind illustrated here with the help of a few models.

4. It may be useful to enlarge on the way models (3a) and (3b) have been simplified. As one may recall, the series of models began with a short account of the possible changes in the *grouping* of the players which may result from an increase in the *number* of players. The way the model begins might give rise to a misunderstanding. If an increase in the number of players is taken as the hypothesis, it is possible to demonstrate certain changes in the figuration relatively simply and clearly. But it does not mean that changes in population, taken on their own, are the main stimulus to social changes. Population changes are changes in the number of people *belonging to particular social units*. The unit of reference in such a population movement may be the whole of mankind or one part of the world, a state or a tribe. Yet without a specific unit of reference the idea of a population movement has no meaning. A population change is not a phenomenon which can occur in a vacuum. It is always just one aspect of a more comprehensive change in a particular social unit. If its population increases or decreases over a particular period, one may be quite sure that there is a change not only in the number of members, but in many other aspects also – in other words, the unit of reference as a whole is changing during this period. But it would be precipitate to conclude that in these circumstances the population shift is the cause and all other changes only its consequences. In this and other instances students of sociology meet with certain difficulties, in that we have been reared in a tradition which leads us to expect to find an explanation for every apparently inexplicable event in a single cause. As already indicated, this habit of thought is not in fact properly suited to helping us comprehend the forms of organization found at the level of integration of human societies. That is also true in this instance. The rapid increase in the population of Europe during the late eighteenth and early nineteenth centuries constitutes both a cause and an effect in the machinery of the overall changes which occurred in European societies during this period. The actual

process of democratization reflected in models (3a) and (3b) is definitely not connected only with the increase in population but with this overall change as well. As a mental experiment, however, it is quite rewarding to ask oneself what kinds of changes in grouping are only possible when there is an increase in the membership of a society.

Digression: an index of the complexity of societies

It is not necessary to discuss whether the subject matter of sociology is more complex than that of the preceding levels of integration – more complex, that is, than the fields of inquiry of biology or physics. It may be useful, though, to give the reader a chance to form an idea of the complexity of human societies.

This can be done fairly simply by asking how much the number of possible relationships within a group increases, when the number of people in the group rises. It is useful to pose this question, even if it does no more than remind us that sociologists' often rather complicated trains of thought are only justifiable and fruitful if they are based on the demonstrable complexity of the field under investigation. They ought not to be merely the product of the researchers' contortions as they try to force their observations of their subject matter into the mould of their preconceived system of thought, which is totally inelastic because of their emotional involvement with it. Sociology is concerned with people; its central issues are their interdependencies. The term 'human relationships' often conjures up ideas of one's immediate, day by day, hour by hour experiences within the cramped circle comprising oneself, one's family and one's job. People are hardly aware of the problem created by the possibility that hundreds, thousands, millions of people may have some relationship to each other and be dependent on each other, although this may well happen in the modern world. Despite this general lack of awareness, the wide span of dependencies and interdependencies which now bind people together are among the most elementary aspects of human life.

Table 1 provides a helpful introduction to this complexity. We need not explore here whatever wider theoretical significance it may possess. In a relatively simple way it enables us to see how quickly it becomes impossible for individual people who make up a network of interrelationships to comprehend it and see their

Table 1 *Increase in number of possible relationships relative to the number of individuals in a web of relationships*[10]

1 Number of individuals	2 Two-person relationships	3 Increase	4 All possible (single) relationships	5 Increase	6 All possible relationships (multiple perspectives)	7 Increase
2	1	–	1	–	2	–
3	3	2	4	3	9	7
4	6	3	11	7	28	19
5	10	4	26	15	75	47
6	15	5	57	31	186	111
7	21	6	120	63	441	255
8	28	7	247	127	1016	565
9	36	8	502	255	2295	1279
10	45	9	1013	511	5110	2815

$$x = \frac{n(n-1)}{2}*$$

$$x = 2^n - (n+1)*$$

$$x = n\left(\frac{2^n}{2} - 1\right)*$$

Examples:
All possible (single) relationships between:

3 people (4) = AB AC BC ABC

4 people (11) = AB AC AD BC BD CD ABC ABD ACD BCD ABCD

5 people (26) = AB AC AD AE BC BD BE CD CE DE
ABC ABD ABE ACD ACE ADE BCD BCE BDE CDE
ABCD ABCE ABDE ADCE BCDE
ABCDE

* In the formulae for the calculation of the numbers of relationships possible in groupings of various sizes, x is the number of relationships (as defined in each case) which individuals can form with one another, and n is the number of individuals in the group.

way through it, let alone to control it. It also enables us to understand more readily the fact that such webs of relationship perpetually effect their own development, relatively independently of the intentions and goals underlying the actions of the individuals who form the web. Since it is sociology's task to make its opacity more transparent, it is important that students of sociology should be aware of this opacity if they wish to understand sociology. This index of complexity is a simple aid. It shows how the possible number of relationships grows as the number of people increases. The former grows fairly slowly, if one takes into account only two-person relationships. But it grows considerably faster if one considers, in purely numerical terms, all the possibilities of relationships involving more than two people. If, rather more realistically, one also takes into account the fact that each participant in what is counted as one relationship has a different perspective on that relationship, one gets a good idea of the increase in complexity accompanying an increase in the number of people making up the web of relationships. The relationship between A and B, man and woman, student and teacher, secretary and boss is, when considered more precisely, not one but two relationships – that of A to B and that of B to A.

But that is not enough. So far we have only taken into account the quantitative aspects of the changes in the number of possible relationships which accompany an increase in the number of individuals in a group. We have not yet taken into consideration the ways in which they may be patterned in the figuration, especially the fact that the balance of power in each of the possible relationships we have considered may vary greatly. We will limit ourselves to illustrating two simple figurational patternings – to the possibility of a relatively even distribution of power and that of a fairly unequal distribution. In the latter case there is a clear relationship of superordination and subordination between individuals. Let us take a four-person relationship as an example. How much does the number of possible relationships increase if we include such differences in figuration in our assessment of complexity, but exclude for the moment the consideration that all relationships also have multiple social perspectives? Here we will limit our deliberations to groups of four people. Column 4 shows eleven possible single relationships for such a group: six two-person relationships, four three-person relationships and one four-person relationship. Taking into account the two possible balances of power mentioned above, there are twice as many two-person relationships (twelve), six times as many three-person relationships (twenty-four) and fourteen times as many four-person relationships (fourteen). Instead of eleven possible single relationships in a four-person group we now have fifty different possible relationships. If in addition we consider the variations in participants' perspectives on relationships, the degree of complexity will rise again. It is certainly not true that all these possibilities will be realized at any given time. But in investigating or merely living in them, we can scarcely fail to consider the range of possibilities, nor to ask which of them actually come about.

The immediate concern here is to make it easier to understand what the task of sociology is. This cannot be done without drawing attention to the opacity and consequent uncontrollability of the intertwining networks of relationship which people form. One of the central problems sociology must set itself is to make these networks more transparent and thereby to prevent them carrying their members along with them so blindly and arbitrarily. This applies above all to intertwining networks which are diffuse and extend over wide space and prolonged time. One question which is difficult to answer is how far people are currently aware of the fact that they themselves form together a functional relationship which stretches right across the world and which, although composed of people, is only very slightly amenable to control by them and accessible to their understanding. There is also the question of how far this situation is distorted by customary explanatory formulae which trace every event either back to individual people or to hostile social belief systems. The indices of complexity set out here may perhaps help to make everyday matters appear rather strange. This is necessary if one is to understand why sociology's field of investigation – the processes and structures of interweaving, the figurations formed by the actions of interdependent people, in short, societies – is a problem at all.

4 Universal features of human society

Mankind's natural changefulness as a social constant

One may investigate how particular human societies differ from one another. One may also investigate how all human societies resemble one another. Strictly speaking, these two research preoccupations are inseparable. Anyone seeking a clear picture of the basic similarities in all societies – the universal features of human society – must be able to draw on a great wealth of knowledge, available in his own society, about the variations possible in human societies. On the other hand, a large quantity of information about the differences between societies may amount to nothing more than a heap of unrelated facts. For it to become anything, an empirically based conception of the *similarities* between all possible societies is essential, to provide a frame of reference within which particular investigations may be carried out. Within the limited framework of this introduction to sociology, it is plainly impossible to accomplish this task satisfactorily. But we can indicate some of the problems, which should make it easier to approach them in greater detail at another time.

This is the more necessary because an approach to these problems demands a radical reorientation of familiar habits of thought. There is nothing particularly surprising about that, if one clearly understands the situation in which people find themselves when striving to gain a better understanding of the societies they form. Centuries of work have provided fairly certain knowledge of how events are interrelated at what is, relatively speaking, the simplest level of integration. This knowledge is symbolized for us by concepts like matter and energy, which, given the present state of knowledge, span the whole range of natural phenomena, from subatomic particles to galaxies. In this field the boundaries of knowledge have been widened and our chances of controlling events have increased at an astonishing rate. The island of secure knowledge which we build for ourselves in the ocean of our ignorance has grown very rapidly, at least in respect of physical nature. Only the human preoccupation with day-to-day happiness, and most of all with misfortunes of the moment, has prevented people forming a comprehensive picture of the development of knowledge and its significance for society, especially for the conception people have of themselves. A similar process is now under way and gaining momentum on the next highest level of integration – the level of organisms. In their practice of scientific effort, if not always in thinking theoretically about it, people are evidently struggling through to the seemingly paradoxical insight that more highly organized nexuses of events may be relatively autonomous from less organized nexuses. The insight is slowly growing that complexes of physical events organized as organisms, plants and animals, possess regularities and structural characteristics which cannot be comprehended merely by reducing them to physio-chemical reactions. In other words, organized units at a higher level of integration are relatively autonomous with respect to events on the next lower level of integration. And distinctive forms of thought and methods of research are needed if scientists are to comprehend correctly the forms of organization of the higher levels of integration.

The same is true of the next highest observable level of integration – that of human societies. Here again, units which considered on their own appear to belong to the previous level of integration are bound together in a functional nexus, but in a completely new way quite different from the way physical units are bound together to form biological units. In the past, societies have often been depicted as though they were really a kind of super-organism. This is because, at first, people's power of conceptual understanding was limited to focusing on the similarities between higher and lower levels of integration. So they were not yet able to grasp the differences upon which their relative autonomy is based.

That is not to imply the idea of an ontogenetic barrier between inanimate and living natural phenomena – or, within the latter category, a barrier between the human and the non-human. It means simply that the effort to achieve *conceptual* mastery of the observable universe results in the insight that the universe is arranged in various levels of integration. After many attempts to bring our means of speaking and thinking into harmony with this observed arrangement, it has become clearer that this is the core of all the difficulties with which we are struggling. In the course of normal scientific feedback from observation to thinking and thinking to observation, the conclusion may be drawn that on this higher level of integration there are forms of organization, types of structure and function, phenomena of the most varied kinds, which differ from those found on the previous level of integration. One may draw other conclusions too: that the phenomena found on the higher level cannot be explained in terms of those found on the lower level; that they are relatively autonomous from them; and that modes of thought differing from those developed for the previous level of integration are required for their understanding. But if one draws these conclusions, one is usually regarded by other people, and may regard oneself, as postulating a break in ontogenetic continuity and thereby a basic division of the universe into two absolutely unrelated spheres, the physical and the metaphysical. In self-defence, one may argue that in the realm of people's socially verifiable experiences – which supply our only reliable information about the world we live in – there are no observations to justify such a division of the world into quite unrelated and absolutely separate levels of integration, such as animate and inanimate matter. But this assertion leaves one open to being misunderstood as implying that the various characteristics of the higher level can be appropriately and adequately explained in terms of events on the low level of integration – or in other words that all phenomena on the higher level can be reduced to those on the lower level. The insight that complete ontogenetic continuity between various levels of integration is compatible with the existence at each level of characteristic and irreducible forms of organization is not immediately self-evident, but, as far as we can see, many advances in biological science, and now in sociology, suggest this. In the last analysis, the autonomy both of the biological sciences relative to the physical, and of the social sciences relative to the biological, are based on the relative autonomy of the respective fields of investigation.

Much points this way. Concepts like birth and death only have meaning in connection with types of integration found at the biological level. There is no equivalent to them on the preceding level, applicable to atoms as well as galaxies, even if transitional forms do occur. (This is yet another illustration of how the concept of integration, as used here, includes particular forms of disintegration – in this case the phenomenon of death –

just as the concept of order has been used in a sense which includes disorder.)

Similarly, in sociology distinct and specific forms of integration and disintegration, patterns of order and disorder, kinds of connectedness, and types of structure and function are encountered which differ from those on all previous levels of integration and cannot be reduced by them, even though the forms found on all levels constitute ontogenetically a single, if subdivided, developmental continuum.

At first sight, the need to delve so deeply just to discuss the universal features of human society may not be quite apparent. But few problems have been treated in so confused a manner as the problem of the relationship of sociology to biology. Over and over again, one encounters tendencies either to reduce sociological problems to biological ones, or to treat sociological problems as though they were completely autonomous and independent of everything that can be said about human organisms. Sociology's autonomy in relation to biology is ultimately based on the fact that people are indeed organisms, but organisms which are unique in certain respects. It is necessary to establish this before the universal features of human society can be discussed. The central, unalterable factor in all societies is human nature. But the uniqueness of man among other forms of life is shown by the fact that the meaning of the word 'nature', when referring to mankind, differs in certain respects from its meaning in other contexts. 'Nature' is usually understood to mean something which will always remain unaltered, something beyond change. One unique aspect of humanity is that human beings are in certain ways changeable *by nature*. A good and serious examination question which is set all too infrequently is 'Which biological characteristics of man make history possible?'. Or, to phrase it in sociologically more precise terms: 'Which biological characteristics are prerequisites for the changeability, and particularly for the capacity for development, shown by human societies?'

There is a wealth of empirical evidence available to answer this question. Yet the question is hardly ever asked, largely because the various human sciences (including both human biology and sociology) pursue their teaching and research not in *relative* autonomy, but in almost *absolute* autonomy from each other. Consequently their theoretical presuppositions are mostly so diverse that they have hardly any point of mutual contact.

During the last two decades there has been a considerable advance in our understanding of the structure of animal societies, and particularly of the nature of bonds between animals. This is mainly the achievement of research by members of the ethological school. But, although it may be contrary to the intentions of the researchers, these and other findings often serve only to underline the differences between animal and human societies. These differences in turn indicate differences between the nature of man and that of animals or, more accurately, differences between the biological constitution of man and that of other organisms. In short, the structure of societies composed of non-human creatures only changes when the biological structure of those creatures alters. Animals of the same species always form societies of the same type, except for very slight local variations. This is because their behaviour towards each other is prescribed by inherited structural characteristics peculiar to each species, which allow only more or less limited scope for modifications. Human societies on the other hand can change without any change occurring in the species – that is, in the biological constitution of man. There is not the slightest reason to suppose that the transformation of pre-industrial European societies into industrial societies was based on a change in the human species. The time-span over which this change took place is too short for us even to consider the idea of a change in the biological structure of mankind. And the same is true of man's social development – from hunters and gatherers to crop-growers and herdsmen or from pre-state tribal groups to the formation of state-societies. It is equally true of many other social changes which, though they have occurred at quite different times, in quite different parts of the world, and as far as we know quite independently of each other, have been in parallel directions.

This is a striking example of the relative autonomy of sociology's field of investigation from that of biology – and therefore also of the difference between the problems of sociology and of biology. Changes in animal societies are aspects of biological evolution. The social relationships of species of animals below the level of man change as functions of the overall biological constitution of these creatures. But the social relationships and behaviour of the species *Homo sapiens* change without there being any change in its biological constitution. This confronts us with the task of discovering the 'nature' – in the sense of 'character' –

of these social changes, and of explaining them without resorting to biological theories. At least, we should resort to them only in so far as they are able to explain how change is possible in human societies, and therefore in the behaviour of individual people and the bonds between them, without there being any changes in man's biological nature.

There is a simple enough answer to this problem. Here we will sketch it only briefly. By nature – by the hereditary constitution of the human organism – human behaviour is directed less by inborn drives and more by impulses shaped by individual experience and learning than is the behaviour of any other living creature. Thanks to their biological constitution, not only is it true that people are better *able* to learn to control their behaviour than any other creature, but also that their behaviour *must* bear the imprint of what they have learned. The behaviour patterns of a human infant not only can but must develop extensively through learning if the infant is to survive. 'Behaviour' means adjustment to changing situations. It is much more efficient, simply from a 'technical' point of view, for it to be guided by individual learning than by mechanisms which are innate and therefore function blindly. The individual learning process operates by the accumulation of experiences in the memory so that they can be drawn upon later to help with the diagnosis and prognosis of any new situation. The extra equipment needed by man for learning has been provided by the development of the hands, the cerebrum and the musculature of face and throat. A decrease or relaxation of behavioural control by blind, automatic, innate impulse is a condition for this development. Evolutionary change in this direction can be traced back through almost the entire animal kingdom, and very clearly through the evolution of mammals. The behaviour of frogs is governed by innate, instinctive reflex mechanisms to a greater degree than the behaviour of the hedgehog or fox, and these to a greater degree again than the anthropoid apes. But even if behaviour in the anthropoid apes is more amenable to modification through learning, and although instincts are correspondingly more easily mollified than in animals at a lower level of biological evolution, these tendencies are still very undeveloped in comparison with those ensured by human biological organization.[1] This is yet another example of the often misconstrued precept, that ontogenetic continuity is perfectly compatible with the emergence of new structures. The anthropoid apes make considerably more varied sounds when communicating with each other, and are considerably more capable of modifying their behaviour by learning, than animals whose organization is that of an earlier stage of evolution. Yet in comparison with the human capacity to vary and modify the sounds they make in social communication, their capabilities are extremely limited. Certain situations trigger the anthropoid ape to make, to some extent automatically and almost unwillingly, sounds like groans, sighs and involuntary laughter. In man these sounds survive in rudimentary form, but superimposed over them as a means of communication are systems of signals. These are not innate, are acquired by learning from other people, and are unique in the animal kingdom. These systems of signals, or languages, are as changeable as the societies which use them as means of communication and cohesion.

A very clear picture of the distinct and specific problems of sociology can be gained by comparing the innate systems of signals on which animals below the evolutionary level of *Homo sapiens* depend, and which can be only slightly modified by learning, with the learned systems of signals, like languages, through which people communicate with each other, and which like human societies are made possible by man's biological organization. The distinguishing features of human social life cannot be understood without reference to the human larynx, oral cavity and tongue, nor to special nervous and muscular equipment, nor to the evolution within the frontal lobes of a region to control the motor abilities for speech. In short, it cannot be understood without taking cognisance of the adaptation of human biological organization for learning. But *because of this biologically determined relative dissociation from biological mechanisms*, and because of the dependence of growing human beings on learning from others, human societies constitute a field of investigation with a type of order and forms of organization different from those which concern biologists. For any discussion of the universal features of human society, three central factors are thus essential. They are: first, relative liberation from non-learned behavioural mechanisms; secondly, the enormous modifiability or changefulness of human experience and behaviour within its own natural boundaries; and thirdly, the constitutional reliance of the human child on learning from other people.

The need for new means of speaking and thinking

The purpose of this section is to reveal more clearly the obstacles which have repeatedly hindered the development of sociology as a relatively autonomous science. The means of speaking and thinking available to sociologists at present are for the most part unequal to the task we ask them to perform. In trying to list the universal features of society, we begin to become aware of the conditions responsible for the relative autonomy of the level of integration represented by human societies. We must now ask ourselves whether the available means of thought and research are sufficiently autonomous from those developed for inquiring into other aspects of reality to be suitable for inquiry into its human and social aspects. For the most part they are unsuitable. In general it is still usual to continue using the tools of communication and thought derived from a particular tradition of speech and thinking, without reassessing them until the point is reached when they have to be discarded as useless. The reason why ways of speaking and thinking are so durable lies in their social nature. In order to fulfil their purpose they must be communicable. When their relative uselessness is recognized and one seeks to develop them further, it is possible to do so only a very little at a time. Unless this rule is observed, words and ideas swiftly lose their communicability.

At first it may perhaps seem that an effort to reorientate our thinking might complicate the work of sociology. But the reverse is true. If this effort is made, the work becomes simpler. *The complexity of many modern sociological theories is due not to the complexity of the field of investigation which they seek to elucidate, but to the kind of concepts employed. These may be concepts which either have proved their worth in other (usually physical) sciences, or are treated as self-evident in everyday usage, but which are not at all appropriate to the investigation of specifically social functional nexuses.*

It may perhaps already have occurred to many readers that there is a need for a substantial reformulation of many aspects of speech and thought about what can actually be observed. Our languages are constructed in such a way that we can often only express constant movement or constant change in ways which imply that it has the character of an isolated object at rest, and then, almost as an afterthought, adding a verb which expresses the fact that the thing with this character is now changing. For example, standing by a river we see the perpetual flowing of the water. But to grasp it conceptually, and to communicate it to others, we do not think and say, 'Look at the perpetual flowing of the water'; we say, 'Look how fast the river is flowing.' We say, 'The wind is blowing', as if the wind were actually a thing at rest which, at a given point in time, begins to move and blow. We speak as if the wind were separate from its blowing, as if a wind could exist which did not blow. This reduction of processes to static conditions, which we shall call 'process-reduction' for short, appears self-explanatory to people who have grown up with such languages. They often imagine it impossible to think and speak differently. But that is simply not so. Linguists have shown that many languages have structures which make it possible to assimilate such experiences differently. The most daring and inspired examination of such limitations in the European tradition of speech and thought is to be found in Benjamin Lee Whorf's book, *Language, Thought and Reality*.[2] He shows that in languages of the European type, sentences are made up of two main elements – substantive and verb, or subject and predicate. In ancient times, these linguistic tendencies were already hardening and becoming systematized, a process furthered by the work of grammarians and logicians of the Aristotelian tradition. It was assumed that this was the universal, the so-called 'logical' and 'rational' way of turning what was observed into thoughts and expressing it verbally. Whorf himself indicates the possibility that such limiting characteristics of our traditional structures of thought and language are partly responsible for the great difficulties encountered by physicists when they try to understand certain aspects of recent research – especially research concerned with atomic particles – and to conceptualize them adequately.

There cannot be the slightest doubt that the same also applies to sociology. Our languages tend to place at the forefront of our attention substantives, which have the character of things in a state of rest. Furthermore, they tend to express all change and action by means of an attribute or a verb, or at least as something additional rather than integral. In many cases this is an unsuitable technique for conceptualizing what we really observe. This constant process-reduction results in the changeless aspects of all phenomena being interpreted as most real and significant. It extends to spheres where it imposes a totally false limitation.

Whorf mentions how we draw involuntary conceptual distinctions between the actor and his activity, between structures and processes, or between objects and relationships. This last tendency in particular is extremely restricting when we are trying to understand human networks; our language tends to compel us to speak and think as though all 'objects' of our thought – including people – were really not only static but uninvolved in relationships as well. Looking through sociology textbooks one finds many technical terms which convey the impression of referring to isolated and motionless objects; yet on closer scrutiny they refer to people who are or were constantly moving and constantly relating to other people. Think of concepts like norm and value, structure and function, social class or social system. The very concept of society has this character of an isolated object in a state of rest, and so has that of nature. The same goes for the concept of the individual. Consequently we always feel impelled to make quite senseless conceptual distinctions, like 'the individual *and* society', which makes it seem that 'the individual' and 'society' were two separate things, like tables and chairs, or pots and pans. One can find oneself caught up in long discussions of the nature of the relationship between these two apparently separate objects. Yet on another level of awareness one may know perfectly well that societies are composed of individuals, and that individuals can only possess specifically human characteristics such as their abilities to speak, think, and love, in and through their relationships with other people – 'in society'.

These few examples may be enough to convince us that we must look critically at inherited structures of speech and thought to see just how useful they are for investigating relationships at the specific level of integration which is human society.

A critique of sociological 'categories'

Such great difficulties would not have to be faced here, had not many of the tendencies in conceptualization just discussed been reinforced and hardened by certain features of the physico-chemical sciences, and by the construction of philosophical theories of science based on them. In the classical period of their development, the aim of research into physical nature was to refer everything which moves and changes back to something static and immutable – that is to say, back to the eternal laws of nature. A philosophical theory of science and knowledge subsequently sanctioned this tendency. To trace back everything observed as mobile and changing to something changeless and eternal was the central task of all science, and the criterion for the scientific status of any field of research. Consequently many academics, especially sociologists, feel a certain disquiet and perhaps even an uneasy conscience: on the one hand they lay claim to being scientists, yet on the other hand they are not in a position to comply with the declared philosophical ideal of science. Closer investigation would probably reveal that, even in the physico-chemical sciences, the search for eternal laws of nature and the reduction of all change to the eternal and unchangeable no longer occupy the same central position they held in classical physics. But for sociologists it is of some importance to demonstrate that the tendency to process-reduction is based on a quite specific value judgement, hallowed by tradition. That anything which changes must be ephemeral, less important, less significant and in short less valuable, passes for almost a self-evident proposition, constantly reinforced by silent consensus.

This scale of values is understandable. It corresponds to people's need for something immortal. But it ought not to be assumed that ways of thinking which accord with this need and with these values are necessarily the most appropriate for facilitating scientific investigation. They need not be most suitable for the investigation of any aspect of the world we live in, least of all that which most concerns us – human society. It can be said unequivocally that both the tendency in science to process-reduction, and the theories of science which raise this to the status of an ideal, have outlived their fruitfulness. It is one of the most remarkable ideas ever thought up by man that any observable change can be explained as the effect of an immovable, static 'First Cause'. A brief, unprejudiced reflection on this must show that one can only trace a motion back to a motion, a change back to a change. That idea may arouse a certain disquiet. Is there then nothing enduring, nothing static? An old philosophical argument asks how we can speak of change unless a Something exists which does not change and which therefore precedes all change.

It can be seen how the patterns of speech discussed above contribute to thought in all these traditional arguments. One must imagine the river to be static before one can say it flows. Are we then not searching for the changeless in ever-changing societies when we talk of the universal features of human society? Not at all. What has been emphasized is that people are *naturally* adapted to change and constitutionally equipped with organs which enable them to learn constantly, to store up new experiences all the time, to adjust their behaviour correspondingly, and to change the pattern of their social life together. Their peculiar changefulness, which has arisen through evolutionary change, is itself the changeless factor at issue here. But this changeability is not the same thing as chaos. It is a special kind of order. Men like Comte, Marx, Spencer and many other classical sociologists of the nineteenth century concerned themselves with investigating this order, the order of change itself. In the twentieth century, the tendency to process-reduction has gradually gained the upper hand in sociology, partly due to a reaction against speculative aspects of classical sociological theories of social change. The pendulum has swung so far in the opposite direction that leading sociological theorists, especially Talcott Parsons, regard stability and immutability as normal characteristics of a social system, and change only as the consequence of disturbances in the normal state of equilibrium of societies. Why the pendulum has swung so far cannot be dwelt upon here.[3] But when a reorientation of sociological thought was mentioned, it was partly intended to convey that the reaction against nineteenth-century evolutionary theories about the order underlying social change has gone all too far in the opposite direction, and remained there much too long. At a time when, in practice, problems of social development are of more acute importance to society than ever before, theories which represent social changes as manifestations of disturbances have robbed us of the possibility of bringing theory and practice into closer contact with each other.

This will require a certain reorientation of sociological thought and perception. At present, sociology is dominated by a kind of abstraction which appears to deal with isolated objects in a state of rest. Even the concept of social change is often used as if it referred to a fixed state – one drifts, so to speak, from seeing the state of rest as normal to seeing motion as a special case. One attains a far better grasp of the raw materials with which sociology deals, if one does not abstract from their motion and their processual character, but rather uses concepts which capture the processual nature of societies in all their diverse aspects, as a frame of reference for research into any given social situation. Similar reasoning applies to the conceptualization of the connection between relationships and the objects which are related. Many technical terms in sociology, in accordance with the tradition mentioned above, are formed in a way which implies that what they seek to represent is an object bearing no relationship to anything else. In other words, present forms of sociological analysis make possible the separation of interrelated things into individual components – 'variables' or 'factors' – without any need to consider how such separate and isolated aspects of a comprehensive context are related to each other. At all events, the relationship appears to be an afterthought, an addition, tacked on later to intrinsically unrelated and isolated objects.

Here too there is a need for reorientation. The special kind of order associated with processes of social interweaving is more suitably dealt with if one starts from the connections, the relationships, and works out from there to the elements involved in them. Our models of the process of interweaving have already shown what kinds of concepts are necessary if people's fundamental relatedness to each other is not to be turned into an abstraction. The same is true of the concept of power. The word 'power' again is usually used as if it referred to an isolated object in a state of rest. Instead we have shown that power denotes a relationship between two or more people, or perhaps even between people and natural objects, that power is an attribute of relationships, and that the word is best used in conjunction with a reminder about more or less fluctuating *changes in power*. That is an example of a concept traditionally based on static components being turned into a concept of relationship.

There are many other examples. For instance, the concept of the individual is one of the most confused concepts not only in sociology but in everyday thought too. As used today, this concept conveys the impression that it refers to an adult standing quite alone, dependent on nobody, and who has never even been a child. In this form the concept has haunted European languages in recent times, and it is echoed in ideas like 'individuality' and 'individualism'. It is found in the theories of many sociologists, who strain themselves in vain to discover how such an 'individual' might be related to 'society', which they conceive as a static entity. Max Weber (1864–1920) – a great sociologist in his intellectual synthesis of empirical data, and a thinker of great insight, for example in his efforts to clarify the basic categories of sociology – never succeeded in solving the problem of the relationship between the two basically isolated and static objects seemingly indicated by the concepts of the single individual and society. Weber axiomatically believed in the 'absolute individual', in the above sense, as the true social reality. He tried to force this belief into a theoretical mould, hoping that sociology might, on this basis, establish itself as a more or less autonomous discipline. But from the start his effort was doomed to failure.

That does not detract from the greatness of his work, nor its importance for sociology. The struggles and conflicts, errors and defeats of great men can play a very important part in the development of a science. But after a while, the errors may obstruct the path. An attentive reader of the classical sociological literature will everywhere find traces of this awkward problem of the relationship between individual and society. Given the prescriptive, static and isolating use of these two concepts, the problem was insoluble. Weber sought to avoid the pitfall in his theoretical work, if not in his empirical, by representing everything which can be said about 'societies' as abstractions without actual reality, and by taking sociology to be a generalizing science. 'State' and 'nation', 'family' and 'army' therefore appeared to him to be 'structures which signify no more and no less than a particular pattern of individual people's social action.'

According to him, abstract sociological statements can never do justice to a multiplicity of individual actions, but they have the advantage of precision. In his theory, Weber broke 'society' down into a more or less disorderly mass of actions by separate, completely independent, self-reliant adult individuals. This attitude forced him into a position from which all observable social structures, types, and regularities had to appear unreal. He could account for typical social structures, such as bureaucratic administrations, capitalist economic systems or charismatic types of domination, only as artificial products of sociologists themselves, as precise, orderly, scientific conceptions, referring to something which in reality is unstructured and unordered.

In his theoretical work, Max Weber was thus one of the great representatives of sociological nominalism; to those inclined to this way of thinking, human society appears to be merely a *flatus vocis*. Emile Durkheim (1858–1917) tended to the opposite way of thinking. He too endeavoured to find a way out of the dead end which is always reached if, in the way just described, one counterposes the concept of the individual to that of society, as two static phenomena. In *De la division du travail social* he wrote:

Of course, it is a self-evident truth that there is nothing in social life which is not in individual consciences. Everything that is found in the latter, however, comes from society. The major part of our states of consciousness would not have been produced among isolated beings and would have been produced quite otherwise among beings grouped in some other manner.[4]

Sociological and other recent literature contains countless examples of this 'chicken-or-egg' problem. Either 'society' or 'the individual' may be valued more highly and so established as real. Or, as Talcott Parsons has attempted, first one and then the other may be established as real (with the 'ego' or 'acting individual' on one side and the 'social system' on the other). But there can be no way out of this intellectual trap as long as both concepts – whether called 'actor' and 'system', 'the unique person' and 'ideal-type', or 'individual' and 'society' – retain their traditional character as substantives, seeming to refer to isolated objects in a state of rest.

Let us first consider the concept of the individual under the microscope. Summoning up the observable facts to which it refers, nothing is found but separate people who are born as infants, have to be fed and protected for many years by their parents or other adults, who slowly grow up, who then provide for themselves in this or that social position, who may marry and have children of their own, and who finally die. So an individual may justifiably be seen as a self-transforming person who, as it is sometimes put, goes through a process – a turn of phrase akin to 'the river flows' and 'the wind blows', as mentioned before. Although it runs counter to our usual habits of speech and thought, it would be much more appropriate to say that a person is constantly in movement; he not only goes though a process, he *is* a process. Then why do scholars so often use traditional concepts like the individual, which makes each person seem like a completely self-reliant adult, forming no relationships and standing quite alone, never having been a child, and therefore never having *become* an adult? The answer is relatively simple. The traditional concept of the individual conveys a mental image. From infancy we are brought up to become independent, perfectly self-reliant adults, cut off from everyone else. We end up believing and feeling we actually *are* what we ought to be and what we may even want to be. More precisely, we confuse fact with ideal, that which *is* with that which *ought to be*.

But this strange dissociation of people as individuals from people as societies cannot be completely accounted for merely by tracing it back to semi-conscious values. Ultimately the roots of the dichotomy lie in a particular way of experiencing oneself, a way which has been characteristic of wider and wider circles of European society since the Renaissance, and which was perhaps occasionally characteristic of a few intellectual élites in earlier times. It leads people to believe that their actual 'selves' somehow exist 'inside' them; and that an invisible barrier separates their 'inside' from everything 'outside' – the so-called 'outside world'. People who experience themselves in this way – as a kind of closed box, as *Homo clausus* – find this immediately obvious. They cannot imagine that there are people who do not perceive themselves and the world in which they live in this way. They never ask themselves which part of them actually forms the dividing wall, and which part is shut away inside it. Is the skin the wall enclosing the true self? Is it the skull or the rib-cage? Where and what is the barrier which separates the human inner self from everything outside, where and what the substance it contains? It is difficult to say, for inside the skull we find only the brain, inside the rib-cage only the heart and vitals. Is this really the core of individuality, the real self, with an existence apart from the world outside and thus apart from 'society' too? People often make use of spatial metaphors which locate them in an undemonstrable position, inside an enclosure which must indeed in some sense be themselves, yet whose existence is difficult to prove. These metaphors express an extremely strong, ever-recurring human feeling, the authenticity of which cannot be doubted. But it is doubtful whether this conception of the self, and this image of human beings in general, corresponds to the facts.

Without pursuing all the problems it raises, it should be said that the image of man as *Homo clausus* is questionable.[5] Here it will be sufficient to point out that it is this mode of self-perception and this image of mankind which lend staying power and conviction to the idea of 'society' existing beyond individuals or 'individuals' existing beyond society. Sociological theorists demonstrate this clearly in their futile struggles with such problems; as Durkheim wrote:

We must, therefore, consider social phenomena in themselves as distinct from the consciously formed representations of them in the mind; we must study them objectively as external things, for it is this character that they present to us. If this exteriority should prove to be only apparent, the advance of science will bring disillusionment and we shall see our conception of social phenomena change, as it were, from the objective to the subjective.[6]

All his life, Durkheim struggled in vain with this problem. In dealing with it, he encountered problems centring on the existence of 'outside' social phenomena in relation to the individual and his 'inner' consciousness, and, closely related to these, a set of older problems in the theory of knowledge, which revolve around the existence of objects 'outside', and their relationship to the individual knowing subject and his 'consciousness', 'mind', 'reason', and other similarly 'inner' attributes. Max Weber tackled the problem differently. But although he was perhaps less explicitly aware than Durkheim of the difficulties, they show through his work no less clearly. For he distinguished between individual actions which are social and individual actions which are not – which are therefore purely 'individual'. From the examples he gave it is plain how questionable this distinction was. According to Weber it is not a social action to open an umbrella when it begins to rain. In his eyes, the action of opening an umbrella is performed without regard to other people. Clearly it never occurred to him that umbrellas are only found in certain societies, and neither manufactured nor used in all. Similarly, he interpreted a collision between two cyclists as non-social; only the insults and blows which might follow were social actions. Weber held that every action directed only to inanimate objects was non-social, though it is plain that different people may attach diverse meanings to a rock, a river or a storm. Thus people in simpler societies with magico-mythical belief systems will ascribe different meanings to these objects, and so their behaviour towards them will also differ from that of people in more secularized industrial societies. One very important formative influence on Max Weber's thought was his feeling that somewhere there must be a borderline or partition between what may be designated as individual and what designated as social. Again it can be seen how far this way of defining the problem has been shaped by the concept of the individual seeming to refer to an apparently static person, rather than to a person who has grown and changed and is still changing, still 'becoming'.

This static person is a myth. If each person is seen as a process, we can possibly say that as he grows up, he becomes increasingly

independent of other people – although this is only true in societies which offer relatively great scope for individualization. But
certainly, as a child, every person has been as dependent on other
people as it is possible to be – he then had to learn from others
how to speak and even how to think. And, as far as we can
ascertain, to small children the feeling of being completely cut
off from other people, or of being secluded 'inside' their own
selves, is quite foreign. Certain difficulties are repeatedly
encountered whenever one tries to arrive at a convincing solution
to the problem of the relationship between that which we call
individual and that which we call society. These difficulties are
certainly closely connected with the nature of the two concepts.
In trying to free our minds from the limitations imposed by the
ideas these concepts foster, the first thing to notice is that they
are based on one simple fact. One concept refers to people in the
singular, the other to people in the plural. After we have put that
into words, this strange way of experiencing ourselves – as if every
single person existed above and beyond every other person –
begins to relax its grip a little. We cannot imagine a person
separate and absolutely alone in a world which is and always has
been devoid of other people. The image of man needed for the
study of sociology cannot be that of a singular person, a *Homo
sociologicus*. Rather it must be that of people in the plural; we
obviously need to start out with the image of a multitude of
people, each of them relatively open, interdependent processes.
All this was implicit in the game models of the last chapter.
From the moment of his birth, every person begins to play games
with other people. Even the tiny child has its trump-cards in
weeping and laughter. But if we are to do justice to the never-
ending process by which everyone is constantly relating to others,
it is necessary to modify the mode of self-experience spoken of
before. We cannot possibly understand the problems of sociology
until we are able to perceive ourselves as people among other
people, and involved in games with others.

Formulating the reorientation in this way, it may seem easy,
perhaps even trivial. But it is not. This way of experiencing oneself as a being whose 'inner self' stands apart from other people
and cut off from 'external things' – meaning 'society' as well as
'objects' – by some kind of invisible barrier is deeply rooted in
highly individualized societies geared to a great deal of intellectual
reflection; so deeply indeed, that we have to make a further

effort of self-distancing before we can grasp the apparently simple idea that every person is one among others, and all the consequences of that idea. Acts of reflection, made as a matter of course by individual members of differentiated societies, imply acts of self-distancing – distancing from the objects of their own thought. As human society develops, people experience themselves increasingly strongly as separate beings, distinct both from other people and from natural objects. Reflection and conscience increasingly interpose themselves through the process of social training as controlling and taming influences between people's own spontaneous impulses to action and other people, other natural objects. So it is anything but easy to combine the insight that the feeling of a dividing line between the 'inner self' and the 'outside world' is very genuine, with the insight that the dividing line is non-existent. *In fact, it requires a further effort at self-distancing.* This is essential if people are to recognize that the apparently real partition between self and others, the individual and society, subject and object, is in fact a reification of the socially-instilled disengagement of their own self-experience.

The personal pronouns as a figurational model

It would be odd if our everyday language did not provide us with means of speech capable of further development along these lines. In fact, people have a whole range of such tools at their disposal. Perhaps it is precisely because they differ from the usual reifying kind of conceptualization that we are insufficiently aware of their potential in scientific conceptualization. One of the most promising models for non-reifying concept formation found in our everyday language is found in the personal pronouns. It is certainly nothing new to use the pronouns for coining concepts in the human sciences. But the earlier ways of doing it demonstrate the strength of the tradition which forces us, when thinking about them, to turn relationships into unrelated static objects. The pronoun 'I' is normally used to communicate to others that a certain statement refers to the person speaking. But in scientific usage it is abruptly turned into a substantive and, given prevailing habits of speech, appears to refer to some independent, isolated person. The concept of ego as used by Freud or Parsons is a good example of how this concept of relationship can be transformed into a concept of substance, a concept of a thing. Parsons's use of the term 'ego' demonstrates the strength of the individual-centred way of thinking. It was quite characteristic that a sociologist like Parsons should remove the lone 'I' from the series of pronouns and contrast it with all other people, although in reality we experience them as 'you (singular), 'he', 'she', 'we', 'you' (plural) and 'they', not as 'alter' or 'the other'. Few features of the type of theoretical sociology recently predominant expose its limitations so clearly.

That the individual positions in this set of relationships cannot be treated separately is easy enough to grasp. The function of the pronoun 'I' in human communication can only be understood in the context of all the other positions to which the other terms in the series refer. The six other positions are absolutely inseparable, for one cannot imagine an 'I' without a 'he' or a 'she', a 'we', 'you' (singular and plural) or 'they'.

The personal pronouns represent the elementary set of co-ordinates by which all human groupings or societies can be plotted out. When communicating directly or indirectly with each other, all people refer to themselves as 'I' or 'we', and to those with whom they are communicating at the moment as 'you'. The third person who temporarily or permanently stands outside the intercommunicating group is referred to as 'he' or 'she', or in the plural as 'they'. Other societies use other signals to enable their members to communicate which of the basic positions in the web of relationships is occupied by the person to whom they are referring. But all human groups seem to have certain standardized symbols for the set of coordinates, which is itself one of the universal properties of human society. It again shows how peculiar are the forms of organization found on the level of integration of human societies. The lower levels of integration have no form of relationship equivalent to the experiencing and grouping of selves as 'I', 'he', 'she', 'you' and 'they'. This form of relationship cannot be traced back to preceding levels, nor explained in terms of them. It illustrates the relative autonomy of societies formed by people with each other, and of the types of communication characteristic of them.

As we have seen, the set of positions to which the personal pronouns refer differs from what we usually have in mind when we speak of social positions as roles – sets of positions like father–mother–daughter–son or subaltern–sergeant–corporal–private. These latter words must, within a given communication, refer always to the same person. Typically in one situation the same personal pronoun may be used to refer to various people. This is possible because the pronouns are relational and functional; they express a position relative either to the speaker at that moment or relative to the whole intercommunicating group. The concept 'I' – the first person pronoun – is symptomatic of the nature of the whole set, indicating the positions held by the communicating people in their relationships with each other. It serves as a means of orientation in a group, whether or not the members are actually present, whether people only refer to themselves as 'I' out loud in the presence of others, or whether they use the concept silently when thinking of themselves. In any case, it must include the idea of other people occupying other positions in the web of relationships to which the set of personal pronouns refers. As we have already said, there can be no 'I' without 'he', 'she', 'we', 'you' or 'they'. It is plainly very misleading to use such concepts as 'I' or ego independently of their position within the web of relationships to which the rest of the pronouns refer.

Taken together, the personal pronouns are in fact an elementary expression of the fact that every person is fundamentally related to other people, and that every human individual is fundamentally a social being. This can be seen very clearly in the awakening of a small child's awareness of himself as a separate person. One's awareness of one's own separate existence is identical with one's awareness of other people existing separately. Understanding the meaning of the *concept* 'I' – which is not always the same thing as the use of the *word* 'I' – is closely linked to understanding what is meant by the concepts 'you' or 'we'. In the development either of single individuals or of whole groups of people, there may be stages during which the conceptual differentiation between different positions in the web of relationships is less pronounced than it is in the linguistic usage of more differentiated societies. It is certainly possible for the symbolic expressions for the first and third persons to be less distinct; to refer to himself a man may use the same symbol as others do – his name. Small children often do this. Nor, probably, are the expressions for the first person singular and plural equally differentiated in all cases; in some societies it may be usual to say 'we' in particular situations where people in other societies would say 'I'. There is great scope here for comparative studies. They may start as purely linguistic studies, but would remain incomplete unless differences in the nature and use of personal pronouns are understood as symptoms of differences in the structure of the relevant groups, their interpersonal relationships, and the way these relationships are perceived. For example, it is interesting to read how and why sets of pronouns of address changed and developed in various European languages.[7]

We cannot, however, explore this wide range of related empirical problems. Our discussion of the significance of the series of personal pronouns leads immediately to an easy transition from the image of man as *Homo clausus* to one of *Homines aperti*. It also helps us to understand something else – that the concept 'individual' refers to interdependent people in the singular, and the concept 'society' to interdependent people in the plural. It may be quite justified and absolutely necessary for scientific work in these two fields to be assigned to different groups of specialists. The first field should be the concern of psychologists and psychiatrists, the second of sociologists and social psychologists. Taking personal pronouns as a model makes it easier to understand that in the long run it is indeed possible to *distinguish* between research into people in the singular and research into people in the plural, but impossible to *separate* them – any more than people in the singular can be separated from people in the plural.

At the same time, this model helps to make clear how inappropriate are certain habits of thought to the human situation. These habits portray the actual 'I' or 'self' as resident somewhere within the individual person, quite secluded from other people, who are addressed as 'you' or 'we', and are spoken of as 'he', 'she', or 'they'. It must be remembered that to perceive oneself as a person of whom one says 'I' involves perceiving other people as 'he', 'she', 'we', 'you' or 'they'. Bearing this in mind may perhaps make it easier to achieve a degree of detachment from the feeling that one exists as a person 'within', and all other people exist 'outside'.

Yet another group of problems, which can be tackled with the help of this model, would remain intractable were only the type of concept-formation currently predominant applied to them. Using concepts which seem to refer to isolated, static objects, it is difficult to do justice to the fact that all relationships between people are matters of perspective. In connection with the index of complexity (see page 101) it has already been suggested that the two-person relationship AB in fact comprises two distinguishable relationships – the relationship AB seen from A's perspective and the relationship BA seen from B's perspective. Working with concepts which make even relationships seem like static objects, it is difficult to do justice to the perspectival nature of all human relationships. The sequence of personal pronouns gives us conceptual raw material to work on which is far better suited to these problems. To begin with, it makes us aware that all the people of whom we speak in the third person speak of themselves in the first, and of us in the third person. The concept of *function* provides a simple example of the perspectival character of human relationships. It is usually employed in connection with *maintaining* a particular social system. Roughly speaking, it is said that a particular institution fulfils this or that function *for* the society. But if we look beyond the reifying use of the concept of institution, to the people who comprise the institution at the time in question, it becomes clear that it is a rather crude simplification to view social functions from a single perspective. This links up with another instance where reification hides the true nature of events. Because the conventional concept of function is substantive in nature, it conceals both the fact that functions are attributes of relationships, and that they are matters of multiple perspectives.

Thus, from the point of view of those who form them, institutions never perform a function exclusively for the so-called 'system', such as a state or a tribe; they also perform a function for their members. To put it another way, they have an 'I-function' as well as an 'it-function'. Either function may be dominant, according to the way power is distributed. In the France of Louis XIV, for example, the office of king performed a function for Louis XIV himself which took precedence over its function for France. As a result of increasing democratization, the function of government posts for a state-society comes to take precedence over their function for those who occupy them, although the latter does not vanish altogether. Unless it takes into account these multiple perspectives, any analysis of social positions and social functions must remain one-sided. It cannot get to grips with what is actually happening. Besides, closer analysis actually shows that, at least in more complex, multi-level societies, the matter does not rest at 'I' (and 'it') functions. Often every pronoun in the series is needed to do justice to the multiple perspectives characteristic of the functions of social institutions.

Max Weber was already on to the track of this problem. Like many of his predecessors, he tried to draw attention to the 'I' and 'we' perspectives on social facts, both in his theoretical work and occasionally in his empirical work too. At the centre of his theory is a challenge to sociologists to work out the *meaning,* the intended sense, which social actions and goals have for the actors themselves. Max Weber himself only solved this problem in part, but he came nearer to success than any of his predecessors. On the whole, sociologists have given this way of approaching the problem less than the attention it deserves. One of the main reasons for this neglect is that without a reasonably precise framework of relationships, such as that provided by the pronoun model, one cannot do justice to the multi-perspectival character of social interconnections.

The pronoun model can be used like this as a set of co-ordinates with reference not only to social functions but to every particular social 'structure' as well. Its advantage is that it enables us to see people again behind all the impersonal, even seemingly extra-human, social structures which so copiously litter the pages of sociological textbooks.

But of course, we cannot simply rest content with defining the perspectives, one-sided as they are for the moment, of players involved in the game. They are indispensable, but on their own they cannot account for the course of the game. It has already been explained how and why the perspectives of individual players intermesh to create a game which no single player can control. On the contrary, it is more likely that the players' moves, plans and perspectives will be influenced by the game. The pronoun model helps us to understand the perspectival nature of webs of human interdependence. In one respect, it makes possible a clearer statement of the sociological problem. Using such names as 'structure', 'system and 'function', people attempt to shed some light from a they-perspective on the paths which games take. But sociologists often have another problem at the same time – of deciding how the participants themselves experience their own moves and the course of the game. Accordingly, sociology must take account of both the first- and third-person perspectives. Similarly, the pronoun model shows that we can never think of people singly and alone; we must always think of them as people in figurations. It is one of the elementary, universal aspects of all human figurations that everyone is interdependent – every person can refer to himself as 'I' and to other people as 'you', 'he' or 'she', 'we' or 'they'. There is no one who is not and has never been interwoven into a network of people, and this is spoken of or thought of by means of concepts based on the pronouns, or by other analogous means of expression. One's conception of such figurations is a basic condition of one's self-conception as a separate person. One's sense of personal identity is closely connected with the 'we' and 'they' relationships of one's group, and with one's position within those units of which one speaks as 'we' and 'they'. Yet the pronouns do not always refer to the same people. The figurations to which they currently refer can change in the course of a lifetime, just as any person does himself. This is true not only of all people considered separately, but of all groups and even of all societies. Their members universally say 'we' of themselves and 'they' of other people; but they may say 'we' and 'they' of different people as time goes by.

The concept of figuration

It is rather unusual nowadays for a book dealing with the problems of society to probe deeply into the notion of the individual, the single person. Scientific specialization is at present so rigorous that to include in a consideration of the universal features of society problems involving people in the singular as well as in the plural, seems almost like illegally infringing a boundary, or even shifting the boundary stones. Perhaps enough has already been said to intimate that the conventional divorce of the scientific study of *the person* from the scientific study of *people* is questionable – but only the divorce, let it be noted, not the distinction between them. One of the most serious shortcomings of conventional sociological theories is that, though admittedly they try to present a clear conception of people as societies, they fail to do the same for people as individuals.

The horizons of sociology are restricted in this way not because these two aspects really form separate subjects, but for the sake of professional compartmentalization. As a result, theoreticians work with a particular well-established conception of the individual, which they never subject to critical scrutiny. For their theories and hypotheses about society, they uncritically take over one of the prescientific conceptions of the person, shot through with all kinds of implicit value judgements and ideals. If this problem is faced fairly and squarely, it is soon apparent that the division between conceptions of the person and conceptions of people in society is an intellectual aberration. The damage which it inflicted on the psychological disciplines need not be closely examined just now. Their theories shine a spotlight on the discrete person, yet how he is embedded in society remains at the shadowy limits of their vision and interest, undiscriminatingly called 'background', 'milieu' or 'surroundings'. Sociologists at any rate should not acquiesce in a tradition which restricts the scope of sociological theories to 'society' alone, which puts ideas about society under the magnifying glass, critically examines them and seeks to reconcile them with other available knowledge – yet does not do the same for ideas about the individual. It goes without saying that one thing cannot be done without the other. When studying mankind, it is possible to shine the full glare of the spotlight first on discrete people and then on to figurations composed of many separate people. Even so, understanding of each level of observation must suffer unless both are constantly considered. Contemporary usage would lead us to believe that the two distinct concepts, 'the individual' and 'society', denote two independently existing objects, whereas they really refer to two different but inseparable levels of the human world.

If we want to introduce new concepts in order to deal adequately with the problem, a certain restraint is necessary. Sometimes scholars take undue advantage of their right to bring new concepts into circulation to express new insights. This may block possible channels of communication, both within the discipline in question and between it and other disciplines. However, given the present state of sociological discussion, there is a specific reason for introducing the concept of 'figuration' here. It makes it possible to resist the socially conditioned pressure to split and polarize our conception of mankind, which has repeatedly prevented us from thinking of people as individuals at the same time as thinking of them as societies. This conceptual polarization is quite clearly a reflection of various social ideals and belief systems. On the one hand there is a belief system whose adherents ascribe the highest value to 'society'; on the other a belief system whose adherents ascribe the highest value to 'the individual'. The resulting idea that two different values correspond to two separately existing objects is becoming fixed in the contemporary conscious-

E

ness. This reinforces the image of the self as 'me in my closed box', and of man as *Homo clausus.*

The concept of figuration[8] therefore serves as a simple conceptual tool to loosen this social constraint to speak and think as if 'the individual' and 'society' were antagonistic as well as different.

The models of processes of interweaving already described in this book make the use of the concept of figuration fairly clear. If four people sit around a table and play cards together, they form a figuration. Their actions are interdependent. In this case, it is still possible to bow to tradition, and to speak of the 'game' as if it had an existence of its own. It is possible to say, 'Isn't the game slow tonight?' But despite all the expressions which tend to objectify it, in this instance the course taken by the game will obviously be the outcome of the actions of a group of interdependent individuals. It has been shown that the course of the game is relatively autonomous from every single player, given that all the players are approximately equal in strength. But it does not have substance; it has no being, no existence independently of the players, as the word 'game' might suggest. Nor is the game an idea or 'ideal-type', constructed by a sociological observer through considering the separate behaviour of each individual player, abstracting the particular characteristics which several players have in common, and deducing from them a regular pattern of individual behaviour. The 'game' is no more an abstraction than the 'players'. The same applies to the figuration formed by the four players sitting around the table. If the term 'concrete' means anything at all, we can say that the figuration formed by the players is as concrete as the players themselves. By figuration we mean the changing pattern created by the players as a whole – not only by their intellects but by their whole selves, the totality of their dealings in their relationships with each other. It can be seen that this figuration forms a flexible lattice-work of tensions. The interdependence of the players, which is a prerequisite of their forming a figuration, may be an interdependence of allies or of opponents.

Taking football as an example, it can be seen that a figuration is a game-structure which may have a hierarchy of several 'I' and 'he' or 'we' and 'they' relationships.[9] It becomes quite apparent that two groups of opponents, who have a 'we' and 'they' relationship to each other, form one single figuration. We can only understand the constant flux in the grouping of players on one side if we see that the grouping of players on the other side is also in constant flux. If the spectators are to understand and enjoy the game, they must be able to understand how the changing dispositions of each side are interrelated – to follow the fluid figuration of each team. Thus it becomes even plainer how senseless it would be to regard each individual player on his own as 'concrete' but the figurations the players form together as "abstract"; or to regard each individual player as 'real' but the grouping of players in their fluid figuration on the field as 'unreal'. Furthermore, it also becomes clear why the concept of power has been transformed from a concept of substance to a concept of relationship. At the core of changing figurations – indeed the very hub of the figuration process – is a fluctuating, tensile equilibrium, a balance of power moving to and fro, inclining first to one side and then to the other. This kind of fluctuating balance of power is a structural characteristic of the flow of every figuration.

These examples may help to convey the meaning of the concept of figuration as it is used here. It can be applied to relatively small groups just as well as to societies made up of thousands or millions of interdependent people. Teachers and pupils in a class, doctor and patients in a therapeutic group, regular customers at a pub, children at a nursery school – they all make up relatively comprehensible figurations with each other. But the inhabitants of a village, a city or a nation also form figurations, although in this instance the figurations cannot be perceived directly because the chains of interdependence which link people together are longer and more differentiated. Such complex figurations must therefore be approached indirectly, and understood by analysing the chains of interdependence. This illustrates again why sociological analysis can never justifiably use de-humanizing substantives as tools of investigation. Such concepts as structure or function, role or organization, economy or culture often fail to convey that they refer to particular figurations of people. The same is true of the concept 'game', if one loses sight of the fact that the game is an aspect of a particular figuration of players.

It is therefore questionable whether sociology can be termed a 'behavioural science', as it so often is. To describe it as such gives the impression that sociological problems would be well on the way to solution if only sociologists concentrated all their attention on the behaviour of the individuals who together make up the social formations in question. Social situations would then seem to be mere abstractions from the common features of the behaviour of many discrete individuals. That is, however, undoubtedly too narrow and distorted a view of the sociological task. Research restricted to the behaviour of many separate people can offer only limited access to problems of social structures, changing figurations of people, the distribution of power or the balance of tensions in figurations, or to many other specifically sociological questions.

This is not to say that there is no place in sociological research for statistical studies dealing with common features in the behaviour of members of certain groups. In many cases they are indispensable. The point at issue is the theoretical hypothesis on the basis of which a statistical inquiry is undertaken. Or in other words, how does the inquiry define the problem which it is seeking to solve? The theoretical framework of figurational and developmental sociology naturally leaves room for statistical inquiry. But, nowadays, statistical requirements often dictate the way sociologists pose their questions. Frequently the type of statistics is one suited only to investigating the behaviour of many separate individuals, surmised to be absolutely independent of each other. To put it colloquially, the tail wags the dog. If sociology has to investigate figurational processes resembling complex games, then statistical aids must be developed which will be suited to this task.

The concept of figuration draws attention to people's interdependencies. What actually binds people together into figurations? Questions like this cannot be answered if we start by considering all individual people on their own, as if each were a *Homo clausus*. That would be to stay on the level of psychology and psychiatry which study the individual person. Indeed, the term 'behavioural science' is derived from them, by way of certain theoretical notions in behaviourism. In other words, all specifically sociological problems are reduced by these means to problems of social psychology. There is a tacit assumption that societies – figurations formed by interdependent people – are fundamentally no more than congeries of individual atoms. The examples of card-games and football matches may help to make the shortcomings of this hypothesis more apparent. The behaviour of many separate people intermeshes to form interwoven structures. The atomic view of society is certainly based in part on an inability to see that these structures, be they marriages or parliaments, economic crises or wars, can be neither understood nor explained by reducing them to the behaviour of their separate participants. That sort of reduction implies a failure to understand the relative autonomy of sociology's field of investigation with respect to that of psychology, and therefore of sociology as a discipline in relation to psychology.

5 Human interdependencies — problems of social bonds

Affective bonds

The concept of figuration puts the problem of human inter-dependencies into the very heart of sociological theory. What makes people bonded to and dependent on each other? This problem is too wide-ranging and many-sided to be treated thoroughly within the confines of this book. People's dependencies on each other are obviously not always the same in all societies at different stages of development. We can, however, try to focus on one or two universal forms of dependence, and to show briefly how people's interdependencies change as societies become increasingly differentiated and stratified.

The opinion is widely held that man's biological characteristics – in contrast to those of subhuman forms of life – play no part in the formation of societies. For example, one type of sociological theory postulates that human norms are essential in integrating society. In fact, this makes it seem as though man's biological equipment made no contribution towards his dependence on other people. Norms are unquestionably not biologically fixed. We have already shown how it is a human characteristic that the grip of inborn forms of behaviour can be relaxed, enabling human societies to develop without mankind developing as a biological species. This too could be taken to mean that man's biological endowments play no part in the formation of his social bonds. If it is simply taken for granted – as it is by Talcott Parsons[1] – that human personality structure is independent of social structure, then it is not surprising that the fact that the human body is a source of 'motivating energies', that it can serve as a 'reward object' yielding 'gratification', is taken as further evidence of the independence of the individual. Parsons is not the only theoretician to take the privacy and individuality of every person's bodily sensations as evidence that man is by nature in effect a self-contained and solitary being. In this case, the conception of man as a lone individual being is so strong that it is often forgotten that each person's striving for gratification is directed towards other people from the very outset. Nor is gratification itself derived entirely from one's own body – it depends a great deal on other people too. Indeed this is one of the universal interdependencies which bind people together.

Moreover, it would certainly be wrong to imagine that this elementary and biologically based dependence on others is confined to the satisfaction of *sexual* needs. There is a profusion of evidence to show that over and above the immediate gratification of their sexual needs, people look to others for the fulfilment of a whole gamut of emotional needs. It is unnecessary here to delve into the question of whether the remarkably diverse and subtle emotional bonds which people enter into with each other are libidinous in origin. There is good reason to believe that people need to be emotionally stimulated by other people even when their sexual valencies are firmly connected in a lasting relationship. This can best be conveyed by picturing a person as having many valencies at any given time. All these are directed towards other people, and some will already be firmly connected with them. But other valencies will be free and open, searching for people with whom to form linkages and bonds. The concept of open emotional valencies which are directed towards other people helps towards replacing the image of man as 'Homo clausus' with that of 'open people'.[2]

This can be illustrated by a simple example. Think of a person who has lost someone he loves through death. This example demonstrates how necessary it is to reorganize our perception if we are to understand the durability typical of elementary emotional bonds between people. When we speak of sexual bonds we are singling out and emphasizing a central but relatively brief and transitory aspect of human relationships. The possibility of emotional durability above and beyond the sexual act is characteristic of human emotional bonds. So is the possibility of there being very strong emotional bonds of many kinds without any sexual overtones.

The categories which were appropriate to research into relatively lower levels of integration are inadequate for research into the human and social level of integration. When a beloved person dies, it does not mean that something has happened in the social 'outside world' of the survivor, which acts as an external cause on his 'inner self'; it will not even do to say that something happened 'there' of which the effect is felt 'here'. Such categories cannot express the emotional relationship between the survivor and the person he loved. The latter's death means that the survivor has lost a part of himself. One of the valencies in the figuration of his attached and unattached valencies had become fixed to the other person. Now that person is dead. An integral part of his self, his 'I-and-we' images, has been broken off.

The valency which had become attached to the other person is torn out. As a result, the particular figuration of all the survivor's valencies is altered and the balance of his whole web of personal relationships is changed. His relationship with another person who had previously occupied only a marginal place in the figuration of his valencies may become much warmer than before. There may be some cooling-off in his relations with others who performed a special function for him in his relationship with the dead person, perhaps by acting as catalysts or as benevolent bystanders. So it would be true to say that when a much-loved person dies, the total figuration of the survivor's valencies and the whole balance of his web of relationships will be changed.

The example draws attention back to everyone's fundamental directedness to other people. In subhuman society this directedness manifests itself in more or less stereotyped and rigid modes of behaviour. In human society these have been lost, but the directedness itself has never disappeared – that is, the deeply-rooted emotional need of every human being for the society of other members of his species. Sexuality is only the strongest, most demonstrative manifestation of this need. Biologically determined instincts are still present, but they can be greatly modified by learning, experience, and the processes of sublimation. There is little justification for regarding the biological constitution of man as something which is relevant only to the 'individual', not to 'society' and to which accordingly no attention need be paid in the study of sociology.

Airing such problems is chiefly important in helping to settle the question of what binds people to each other and forms the foundation of their interdependence. Sociologists are accustomed to looking at human bonds mainly from the 'they' perspective. For example, it is possible to do as Durkheim did and view human bonds chiefly in the context of increasing job specialization, which makes people more and more dependent on each other. These insights are important, but the bonds to which they refer are still merely economic. It is impossible, however, to deal adequately with the problem of people's social bonds, especially their emotional ones, if only relatively impersonal interdependencies are taken into account. In the realm of sociological theory a fuller picture can be gained only by including personal interdependencies, and above all emotional bonds between people, as agents which knit society together.

The significance of these personal aspects of human bonds may not be entirely clear if the only illustration used is that of a single person's nexus of relationships. Nevertheless, it is essential to return to this one person's web of personal relationships, to see how it appears from his point of view – how it feels from the 'I' perspective. This alone makes it possible to understand a whole range of more widely spreading interdependencies based on personal emotional bonds. In small social units containing comparatively few people, every single person's web of personal relationships may include all the other people in the unit. The figuration of each person's attached and unattached valencies will certainly differ from that of everyone else. Yet as long as the unit is small, the figuration will include the whole tribe. As social units become bigger and more stratified, new forms of emotional bond will be found. As well as interpersonal bonds there will be bonds connecting people to the symbols of larger units, to coats of arms, to flags and to emotionally-charged concepts.

In this way, people are emotionally bound together through the medium of symbols. This kind of bond is no less significant for human interdependence than the bonds created, as mentioned above, by growing specialization. The emotional valencies which bind people together, whether directly by face-to-face relationships or indirectly by their attachment to common symbols, form a separate level of bonds. Blended with other more impersonal types of bond, they underlie the extended 'I-and-we' consciousness, which hitherto has always seemed indispensable in binding together not only small tribes but large social units like nation-states encompassing many millions of people. People's attachment to such large social units is often as intense as their attachment to a person they love. The individual who has formed such a bond will be as deeply affected when the social unit to which he is devoted is conquered or destroyed, debased or humiliated, as when a beloved person dies. One of the biggest gaps in the older theories in contemporary sociology is that they mostly investigated the 'they' perspectives of society, hardly ever using precise conceptual tools to investigate the 'I-and-we' perspectives.

Political and economic bonds

Most sociological statements today refer primarily to societies which are organized as states or tribes. Yet it is hardly ever justifiable to select these particular types of society as the basis for everything that is said about 'society' or social systems *in general.* Why not choose the village or the town as a model of society, or (as was often done in the nineteenth century) human society as a whole? What makes complexes like states and tribes so important that it is almost taken for granted that they are what is meant whenever reference is made to social 'wholes'?

In trying to answer such questions, the first point to make is that states and tribes are to a considerable extent objects of common identification – objects to which many individual valencies are bonded. Yet why do emotional bonds to state-societies – which nowadays are nation-states – take priority over bonds to other figurations? At other stages of social development, towns, tribes or even villages have taken priority in the same way. What are the common features of the various figurations which at different stages of development have bound individuals to them by this type of predominating emotional bond?

First of all, these units all seem to have exercised comparatively strict control over the use of physical violence in relationships between their members. At the same time, they have allowed, and often encouraged, their members to use physical violence against non-members. *To date, sociology has lacked any clear conception of the common features of this type of solidaristic grouping at different levels of social development.* Its function is obvious: it knits people together for common purposes – the common defence of their lives, the survival of their group in the face of attacks by other groups and, for a variety of reasons, attacks in common on other groups. Thus the primary function of such an alliance is either physically to wipe out other people or to protect its own members from being physically wiped out. Since the potential of such units for attack is inseparable from their potential for defence, they may be called 'attack-and-defence units' or 'survival units'. At the present stage of social development they take the form of nation-states. In the future they may be amalgamations of several former nation-states.[3] In the past they were represented by city-states or the inhabitants of a stronghold. Size and structure vary: the function remains the same. At every stage of development, wherever people have been bound and integrated into units for attack and defence, this bond has been stressed above all others. This survival function, involving the use of physical force against others, creates interdependencies of a particular kind. It plays a part in the figurations people form, perhaps no greater but also no more negligible than 'occupational' bonds. Though it cannot be reduced to a function of 'economics', neither is it separable from it.

Given the range of his experiences, a nineteenth-century European might be expected to perceive the immediate danger of people starving to death as a result of unequal distribution of power within a state, while the risk of being subjugated or killed by an external enemy might seem to him only marginal. So Marx was a man typical of his age in perceiving, albeit more sharply and clearly than anyone before him, the interdependencies arising out of the division of labour in the production of means of subsistence and other goods. In consequence he was also able to grasp more clearly than his predecessors the structure of the conflict associated with the monopoly of the means of production by certain groups. Yet it was equally typical that he should fail to perceive that the danger of one group of people being subjugated or physically annihilated by another was highly significant as a basis for certain kinds of integration and interdependence. Marx observed a particular stage in the development of industrial society. Corresponding to this stage was his belief that the functions and power resources of the state could be explained as deriving from the functions and power resources of the bourgeois entrepreneurial groups. Ultimately he believed that they derive also from the class interests of those social groups to whom we owe the meaning of the concepts of 'the economy' and 'economics'. For at the time Marx was writing it was still a relatively new idea that certain forms of interdependence – those most closely connected with the specialized business activities of the entrepreneurial strata – possessed laws of their own and were to some extent autonomous with respect to all other social activities. This sphere of activity was described by the then relatively new term 'the economy'. On the one hand, the recognition of its autonomy was associated with the development of the new science of economics. On the other hand, the theoretical exposition of the autonomy of 'economic' functional nexuses and their autonomy within the overall context of a state-society was most closely linked with the demand of the wealthy and rising English middle classes for freedom from state intervention in their own enterprises. They demanded that 'economic' laws – the free play of supply and demand – should be allowed to take their own 'natural' course.

To the rising entrepreneurial bourgeoisie, struggling to free itself from intervention by governments whose members were still drawn mainly from the pre-industrial aristocracy, it may indeed have appeared that the 'economy' possessed absolute functional autonomy from the 'state'. This idea found symbolic expression in the development of the nascent science's name. From 'political economy', symbolizing that the economic sphere is a subdivision of the political, was derived 'economics', the symbolic expression of the idea that as society develops, an independent economic sphere emerges with immanent, autonomous laws of its own. The claim of the bourgeois entrepreneurs that the 'economy' *ought* to be autonomous and free from state intervention became metamorphosed. From it developed the idea that the economy, as a sphere within the functional nexus of a state-society, actually *was* quite autonomous. This set of liberal ideas was clearly reflected in Marx's conception of the relationship between the economy and the state. It led him to think of the 'economic' sphere as an autonomous self-contained functional nexus with laws of its own, but within the functional nexus of the whole society. Both the entrepreneurial bourgeoisie and the science of economics claimed that the state obviously *ought* to be an institution for the protection of bourgeois interests. Accordingly, Marx depicted the organization of the state as though it actually did nothing but that, and had no function other than defending bourgeois economic interests. In other words, he took over an ideology derived from the bourgeois science of economics, changing its sign, so to speak, from plus to minus. From the point of view of the working class, the defence of bourgeois interests seemed pernicious; therefore the organization of the state must seem pernicious too.

Analysed more closely in the light of developmental sociology,[4] it is clear that the development of political and economic structures were two quite inseparable aspects of the development of the whole functional nexus of society. Closely associated with the development of political institutions were many processes leading to the lengthening of chains of social interdependence. Among these processes were the growing 'economic' division of labour and the superseding of limited local markets and enterprises as nodal points of the social network by much larger ones. The institutions of the state were capable of guaranteeing the safety of traders and their goods, now transported over longer and longer distances, of ensuring that contracts were fulfilled, of levying import duties to protect infant industries from foreign competition, and much besides. In their turn, the development of political institutions was closely associated with the spreading networks of trade and industry. From a sociological point of view, the development of the state and political organization and of the occupational structure were indivisible aspects of the development of one and the same functional nexus. In fact, these so-called separate 'spheres' of society are none other than the integrating and the differentiating aspects respectively in the development of the same web of interdependence. Every so often, the functional differentiation of society lurches forward, outstripping the development of the integrating and coordinating institutions of the time. In the industrialization of England, the great leap forward just before and after 1800 is an example of how processes of differentiation can overreach themselves in this way. The corresponding development of coordinating institutions was notoriously slow. This situation became intellectually enshrined in the idea that the 'economic sphere' can be regarded as the engine of all social development. However, the development of the economy without corresponding development of the state and political organization is as unthinkable as the latter without the former, since both are part of developing webs of interdependence. The conceptual separation of these two spheres, and the absolute autonomy of the respective social sciences dealing with them, are a leftover from the period defined 'ideologically' as that of economic liberalism. Sociologically speaking, that was, as we have said, *a period during which the functional differentiation of chains of interdependence outpaced the corresponding process of integration.* If, instead of the traditional model of 'spheres', one of increasing or decreasing functional differentiation and integration is used, an immediate advance is made. It leads to a sociological conception of society, displacing the extremely artificial image of society as a hotch-potch of adjacent but unconnected spheres, of which first one and then another is singled out as the true driving force behind social development.

Both the theoretical and the practical effects of correcting these habits of thought will be far-reaching. At this point we need mention just one implication. As long as the 'economic sphere' is pictured as functioning more or less autonomously in and for itself within the overall context of the state-society, social stratification is liable to be portrayed in terms of this separation of spheres. Thus stratification in industrial societies is seen in terms of social classes and their conflicts of interest, which are determined primarily by economic factors. This conception corresponds fairly accurately to the grandstand view of the strata which are themselves involved. From this perspective it appears as if their power struggles are simply about the distribution of economic chances, about the changing balance between wages and profits.

Yet here, too, closer study reveals the inadequacy of the idea that the tensions and conflicts between the two great classes in industrial society – the industrial working class and the industrial bourgeoisie – can be explained by focusing on 'economic' chances to the exclusion of all the other chances subject to dispute. When compared with what can actually be observed, this is plainly misleading. On closer examination, the problem appears to concern the distribution of power throughout the length and breadth and on every level of multi-level industrial state-societies. For example, one of its aspects is the distribution of power chances on the level of the individual factory. Which groups in factories have access to positions of command, carrying responsibility for coordination and integration? And which groups do not? People occupying the position of employer are interdependent with people in the position of worker, because of the particular functional relationship between the two positions. But their reciprocal dependencies are not the same – the power weightings are not equally distributed. Even at this level, the problem does not merely concern how the income available in the business for sharing amongst the groups occupying various positions is actually divided between them. The distribution of these 'economic' chances is itself a function of the greater balance of power – the distribution of power chances between these groups. The balance of power within an industrial concern is not, however, expressed solely in the distribution of 'economic' chances, but also through the distribution of chances for the members of one of these groups to control, command and dismiss the others in the course of their work.

Bearing in mind the distribution of power between capitalists and workers which Marx witnessed in the England of the first half of the nineteenth century, it is quite understandable that he paid almost exclusive attention to analysing the distribution of economic chances. A considerable part of the labour force was living at bare subsistence level. The workers were minimally organized at factory level and even less at the higher levels of the national state. In any case, Marx's concept of class applied to only one level. As he saw it, the only point of contact between working and capitalist classes was in the places of production; their contact was solely the result of the nature of their positions in the production process. In his day, workers and employers never met on any other level, since neither group had any effective unifying organizations on higher levels of integration in society, let alone any national or party organizations. So it was understandable that his conception of class referred only to specific groups of positions in the production process. Nor has this analysis lost its relevance as industrial societies have developed further. But now it can be seen more clearly that the analysis, though indispensable, is incomplete. Even in Marx's time, the balance of power in the factory between workers and employers was not completely self-contained; it did make some difference whether, or how far, the then agents of the state cast their weight into the scales for the benefit of one side or the other. As industrial societies have developed, the trend has been for the importance of disputes, skirmishes, compromises and settlements at the factory level to decline relative to those at higher levels of integration, notably in the most central institutions of the state, like parliament and the government.

It is therefore necessary to correct the traditional one-level conception of class seemingly based entirely on the distribution of economic chances. A conception of class is needed which takes into account the fact that functionally and organizationally interdependent disputes between workers and employers are enacted on many levels of integration other than that of the factory. They are acted out especially at the highest level of integration of a state-society. This new conception must take into account that in all the more developed societies the two organized classes are nowadays far more integrated into these state organizations than they were in Marx's day. In fact both these industrial classes have become ruling classes, because they are represented on all the various levels of integration of industrial society – on the local and regional as well as the national level. The distribution of power between the two classes is still very unequal, especially at factory level, but not as unequal as in Marx's day. And tensions of a new kind are emerging alongside those which Marx noted at a time when these social classes could still be regarded as homogeneous, one-layer social formations at factory level. These new tensions occur between the rulers and the ruled, and do not preclude tensions between people who represent the same class at different levels of integration.

The often neglected relationship of processes of integration and differentiation is very useful in studying long-term social change. These processes are not so complicated as they often appear. This is an example of how difficulties are due more to theoretical confusion than to the complexity of the subject matter itself. There is a whole range of relatively simple possibilities for analysing long-term processes of social integration and differentiation. When considering integration, one possibility is to ascertain the number of hierarchically graded levels of integration found in the societies being structurally analysed. It will be found that if different societies have the same number of levels, they will also have other structural similarities. There are equally simple methods of analysing stages of differentiation. One is to determine the number of occupations for which a society has distinct names. Of course, this source material is not always available or accessible, but many of the sources which are available have not yet been tapped.

This simple method of determining with greater precision the stage the division of labour has reached at a given time throws a curious light on what we rather one-sidedly designate 'processes of industrialization'. Compared with every kind of pre-industrial society, and especially with medieval societies, the number of occupational groups distinguished by name in industrial societies is astounding. Not only that, but the number increases at a rate unknown in earlier times. For the individual, the significance of this is that he becomes caught up in ever-lengthening chains of interdependence which for him constitute functional nexuses beyond his control. At the same time it means that, in comparison with earlier societies, power chances will be less unevenly distributed, and that the reliance of interdependent positions on each other will become relatively less one-sided and more reciprocal. Yet it also means that as functional differentiation makes people on many levels interdependent, they simultaneously become more dependent on the centre for their coordination and integration. People who have access to and who occupy coordinating and integrating positions will clearly have great power chances at their disposal. Consequently, though integrating and coordinating social positions are indispensable, one of the main problems in highly differentiated societies is how to maintain effective institutional control over them. How can it be socially guaranteed that the occupants of such positions do not to any great extent subordinate their 'it' and 'they' functions to their own purposes?

The development of the concept of development

When people in the second half of the twentieth century talk about the 'development' of societies, they are generally using the concept in relation to quite clearly defined practical problems. It is mostly used in speaking about 'developing countries' whose governments are each striving with varying degrees of energy, but usually with the assistance of richer and more powerful societies, to develop their own particular country. In this sense 'development' means an activity, something which people do with clear aims in mind and with a certain amount of planning. In its essentials, the great aim of this planned development is simple enough: to ameliorate the relative poverty of such societies. Ways and means are sought to raise the income of the ordinary people, and not to increase the wealth of just a few persons – for in most poor countries there are usually some extraordinarily rich individuals, often richer than in generally better-off countries. In the face of such concrete problems, philosophical frivolities – whether 'society' has an 'existence' above and beyond the individual, whether society is anything other than an abstraction from the behaviour of many separate individuals, or whether 'individuals' can possibly exist without societies or 'societies' without individuals – are overshadowed. Obstacles to understanding that societies are figurations of interdependent people are swept away when we are confronted with the problems of the 'developing countries'. In seeking to develop these societies and alleviate the poverty of the whole people, not just of some of its members, the need is for decisive measures to regulate the productivity and income of all individuals who are politically integrated within a particular state.

'Development' in this sense appears to be primarily an activity carried out by people. It is implemented chiefly by people holding government posts and their helpers, development experts from 'more advanced' countries. Especially in the eyes of the latter, development appears to be an 'economic' problem. They strive to raise the 'economic potential' of these poorer state-societies. They try to increase the capital stock. They build power stations, roads, bridges, railways and factories. They endeavour to boost agricultural productivity. But when specifically economic 'development' is set under way like this with the limited aim of improving the standard of living, it becomes evident that it is impossible to develop economic potential without a total transformation of society. Purely economic plans may fail because other non-economic but functionally interdependent aspects of a society act as a brake by pulling in the opposite direction. It is possible that the 'development' which was consciously directed towards economic transformation may set in motion development of a quite different kind not intended by the government making the plans. If government activity in planning development, which constitutes intentional human action, can be described conceptually by means of a verb, then a more impersonal expression is needed for these social changes neither deliberately initiated nor controlled by planners or actors. Planned actions in the form of government decisions may have unanticipated, unintended consequences. Rather optimistically Hegel called this 'the cunning of reason'. It is now more obvious that these unplanned consequences of planned human actions arise from their repercussions within a web woven by the actions of many people. In making this idea explicit, a concept of action becomes a concept of function. Instead of speaking of people acting to develop societies, we have to speak more impersonally of the process of development.

Though it is unplanned and not immediately controllable, the overall process of development of a society is not in the least incomprehensible. There are no 'mysterious' social forces behind it. It is a question of the consequences flowing from the inter-meshing of the actions of numerous people, the structural properties of which have already been illustrated by means of game models. As the moves of thousands of interdependent players intertwine, no single player nor group of players acting alone can determine the course of the game, no matter how powerful they may be. What in Chapter 3 was described as 'the course of the game' is encountered here as 'development'. It involves a partly self-regulating change in a partly self-organizing and self-reproducing figuration of interdependent people, the whole process tending in a certain direction. We are dealing with states of balance between two opposing tendencies towards self-regulation in such figurations: the tendency to remain as before and the tendency to change. They are often, but not always nor exclusively, represented by different groups of people. *It is perfectly possible that by their own actions, groups of people consciously orientated towards preserving and maintaining the present figuration in fact strengthen its tendency to change. It is equally possible for groups of people consciously orientated towards change just to strengthen the tendency of their figuration to remain as it is.*

Prevailing theoretical hypotheses still give precedence to tendencies towards persistence. One is inclined to consider it 'normal' that a society should linger in the state it has attained, so long as defects and deviations from the norm leave its equilibrium undisturbed. This is easy to understand as the expression of an ideal, particularly in a period when all conditions of life are in a state of flux, which it appears no one can control. 'Where is order to be found, if at all, amid the relentless flux?' wrote one researcher concerned with this kind of economic problem.[5] But perhaps the real reason why social development remains so puzzling to us is that our efforts are directed less towards understanding and explaining what actually happens and to making a diagnosis, than towards making a hopeful prognosis.

Yet it is anything but easy to grasp the significance of understanding the concept of 'development' more as one of function than one of action. In everyday life it may no longer be very difficult to appreciate what is meant by 'society is developing'. Because enough people have the necessary conceptual equipment, the word 'development' now communicates the idea of a relatively impersonal and spontaneous social transformation. Two hundred and fifty or three hundred years ago, however, this could not be assumed. Even the most highly educated and learned of men in those days were unable to grasp intellectually the conception of 'development' which is nowadays taken for granted. The verb 'to develop' and its derivatives were used only to express certain human actions – for example, as the opposite of 'to envelop'. The only remaining trace of this older meaning of the word is in its application to films. When we talk about 'developing' them we are using a concept only of action. We develop the hidden picture. In earlier times one could in the same way speak of developing a hidden secret. Neither the concept nor the mental image now associated with the word 'development' was available to people of earlier times.

But, it may be asked, did they not see that children develop into adults? Did they not see that their own society was developing all the time? No, they were unable to see, they never saw. They could not conceptualize what they 'saw' in the same way that we do and thus were unable to perceive it in the same way. Eventually the concept of development was recast, so that it became associated with an impersonal sequence of events, which was to a large extent self-regulating and tended in a particular direction. But this transformation required many generations of thought, and a continuous, cumulative increase in the stock of social experience and of concepts, with continuous feedback between them.

For a long time it was extremely difficult for people to imagine that such a chain of events, whether largely under control or not, might be both orderly and unplanned, structured yet unintentional. One reason for their difficulties was that this conception did not correspond to the questions they asked about events, the questions which interested them. It stood in direct opposition to prevailing values and belief systems. A much clearer insight is gained into the meaning and function of the concept if one realizes the difficulties which stood in its path. Perhaps *the* major obstacle to conceptualizing certain observable changes as 'development' had to do with what people anticipated when they asked questions about these observable changes. The crucial aim underlying all fundamental questions asked about things which they observed to be changing was the discovery of something immutable in or behind all changes. The only satisfactory answer to queries about observable change would be one which made reference to some ultimate goal. People always pose their questions in ways which conform to their hypothesis as to what constitutes a satisfactory answer. So, at that time, questions were framed in such a way that from the outset attention was drawn to the purpose underlying the question. The questions were shaped so that they might disclose the 'essence', the 'basic principle', the 'fundamental law', the 'first cause', the 'ultimate goal', or some other explanation thought to be eternal and immutable. People wanted to know what lay beneath the ever-flowing stream of events. Again there were predetermined evaluations at work. A higher value was implicitly placed on the changeless than on the changeable. So it was taken for granted that in the pursuit of knowledge, the latter should be traced back to the former. Mankind had to tread a long and laborious route before people succeeded in first slackening the grip of this dominant scale of values, enmeshed as it was in the whole search for knowledge, and finally breaking it altogether in several fields of inquiry. This story cannot be retraced here in full, but it may be possible to convey that this scale of values, and its attendant patterns of thought, methods of research, and types of question, were not based on any deliberate examination of their suitability for their field of investigation. Rather they were based on the needs of the people asking the questions – needs of the kind expressed in the question quoted earlier: 'Where is order to be found, if at all, amid the relentless flux?' Order in this sense must *eo ipso* mean something unchanging, which helps people intellectually to escape the disquieting flow of events.

From the second half of the eighteenth century onwards, after many false starts, there began a gradual shift in the evaluation of changeable phenomena. At first this shift was confined to limited areas where scientific knowledge was making progress. Certain social changes, some of which have been mentioned earlier – in particular, the demand for social change during and after the French revolution, the operation of market mechanisms in conditions of relatively free trade, and scientific progress – liberated people's powers of imagination and enabled them to perceive relationships which had no place in the traditional schema. People acquired the capacity to conceive of an order which was not detected by tracing all change back to something changeless, but which showed itself rather as an immanent *order of change*. People began to discover in nature, as well as in society, changes which could not be explained in terms of external substances or immutable causes. Scientific questions were gradually reorientated away from searching for the unchangeable to searching for an immanent order of change. The best known example is how the static Aristotelian and later Linnaean classification of organisms turned gradually into the Darwinian idea of an evolutionary order. The gist of that idea is that, with a few regressions, more complex and differentiated forms of life develop blindly and purposelessly out of less complex, less differentiated forms of life.

The difference between Aristotle's and later Montesquieu's conception of society on the one hand and that of Comte, Spencer and Marx on the other, is a further example of this reorientation. The latter ascribed great importance to the question of the immanent order of change. Certainly they had forerunners, but more than ever before, the founders of sociology championed the general idea of social change, and they did so with closer reference to empirical evidence of one kind or another. The theories of development put forward by the great sociologists of the nineteenth century were only a step in the right direction; and, as we now know, it was followed in the twentieth century by a step in the opposite direction. But as scientists began to turn away from reducing observed changeability to imagined immutability, a great stride was made towards rendering the tools of human thought more appropriate to observable relationships.

In the twentieth century, an extraordinarily strong reaction set in against the developmental theories of nineteenth-century sociology. The knowledge on which nineteenth-century sociologists had to rely was very limited in comparison with the growing mass of separate pieces of knowledge about the development of human societies now available to anyone interested. It was thus much easier for them to perceive a clear trend in the development of society. Their capacity for perception had not yet been swamped by the mass of detail which must now be taken into account in any comprehensive model of development. They saw the wood more clearly than the trees – which is just what we are scarcely able to do. It often seems that the mass of information now available will not fit into any unified scheme of social development.

It certainly will not fit into the synoptic models of social development which have been handed down to us by the great nineteenth-century pioneers of sociology. Yet it was precisely because these pioneers were not weighed down with too many bits of information, nor aware of the gaps in their knowledge, that they were able – in all innocence and very fruitfully too –

to fill in the gaps with inspired speculation, influenced in the main by the acute social problems of their age. Almost all the nineteenth-century pioneers of developmental sociology were obsessed with the problem of a new and better social order which they hoped and believed would come about in the not-too-distant future. They took it as axiomatic that the future condition of mankind must be better than in their day. As a kind of social religion they shared the belief that society develops and progresses at a steady pace. Their ideas about the direction of this steady progress varied greatly, however, in accordance with the diversity of their social and political ideals. Marx's idea of progress was very different from that of Comte, whose idea was different again from Spencer's. But they shared the understanding that society was developing more or less 'automatically' towards a better social order. They valued certain elements in past social development more highly than others, their main criterion being their ideal of the better social order that was to come. In this sense all sociological theories of the nineteenth century had strong teleological overtones; they lapsed into the old notion that all change occurs within a more or less changeless context. Even Marx was unable to free himself completely from the idea that the victory of the proletariat would do away with the chief cause of social development – the class struggle and the internal contradictions within society – and that social development in its known form would then also cease. Thus, pursued to their logical conclusion, these ideas about change led to the idea of society in its ultimate immutable state; an idea of the ideal realized which was the final yardstick or point of reference.

This constant mingling of factual references with social ideals in the models of social development constructed by the great nineteenth-century sociologists, is undoubtedly one of the reasons why for a long time twentieth-century sociology failed to take them into account in its modern theories of social development. Sociological thought shifted away from a concern with the long-term dynamics of societies to a concern with relatively short-term problems, especially those of immediate and present-day social conditions. The decisive factor in this shift was not so much any criticism of classical models of development, but rather that twentieth-century sociological theories have been shot through with social and political ideals which place the highest value on certain *existing* societies. Perhaps the baby was thrown out with the bath water. Because they were opposed to the ideals implicit in classical sociological models, people rejected out of hand many fertile products of classical sociological thought, including a concern to investigate social change as *structured* change.

In accordance with ideals centred on certain present-day societies, sociological theoreticians have turned their attention to constructing models of society in a state of rest – models of 'social systems'. In so far as they are still occupied at all with problems of long-term social development, they try to master them by reducing them first to various phases in social development and finally to static types like 'feudal society' and 'industrial society'. Leading sociological theoreticians have simply abandoned the question of how societies moved from one phase to another as they developed. Immutability is treated as the normal condition of society. It is embedded in such basic sociological concepts as 'social structure' and 'social function'. Problems of social change now appear supplementary, and have a chapter to themselves, entitled 'Social Change'. No immanent order is ascribed to social change itself. There has been a revival of the old idea that changes must be traced back to something changeless, constituting the actual structured 'regularities'. The nineteenth-century classical sociologists' great advance towards recognition that change itself has an immanent order and structure has now been lost. That does not mean to say that 'order' is synonymous with 'consensus' or 'harmony'. 'Order' simply denotes that the sequence of change is not 'disorderly' or 'chaotic'. It means that it is possible to discover and explain how later social formations arise out of earlier ones. That is the essential problem for 'developmental sociology'.

Social values and social science

Even now, sociological investigation, especially at the theoretical level, has achieved remarkably little autonomy with respect to the great social belief systems by which people orientate themselves in the face of crises and upheavals which they find almost wholly opaque and inexplicable. As is apparent from the fate of the concept of 'social development', the development of the science of sociology itself has been bound up with shifts in the distribution of power and struggles between the great social belief systems.

Everyone concerned with sociology must ask himself the following questions. First, in constructing or criticizing sociological theories, to what extent am I primarily attempting to establish the validity of a preconceived idea of how human societies *ought* to be ordered? Secondly, to what extent do I accept those results of theoretical and empirical investigations which confirm my own aims and hopes, and disregard those which are incompatible with them? And, thirdly, to what extent am I chiefly concerned to find connections between particular social events, how their sequence can actually be explained, and what help sociological theories can offer in explaining and determining the trend of social problems – and, last but not least, in providing practical solutions to them?

Underlying this book is an unambiguous answer to such questions. The sociologist should not be required or expected to express his convictions about how society *ought* to develop. Sociologists ought rather to free themselves from the notion that there is or even will be any necessary correspondence between the society they are investigating and their own social beliefs, their wishes and hopes, their moral predilections or their conceptions of what is just and humane.

This attitude to the treatment of sociological problems is based on a conviction that it is neither relevant nor permissible to intermingle and confuse these two issues. Sociology and ideology have quite different functions. Some people claim that it is impossible to keep one's preconceived personal convictions apart from one's theoretical, scientific and sociological approach to problems. They claim that everyone mixes the two, that we are all engaged and involved. They are quite clear about the tacit assumptions they are making when they speak out in favour of mingling theory and value in social science. They implicitly assume a kind of pre-established harmony between social ideal and social reality. This view roughly corresponds to ideas about nature often found in the seventeenth and eighteenth centuries. The notion then predominated that nature is fundamentally organized in such a way that people will find it reasonable, useful or good. Similarly many of sociology's theoreticians take it for granted that human societies develop in accordance with their own values, and thus spontaneously take shape in a way which seems significant to them.

No such assumption is implicit here. Over a long time-span, social sequences proceed blindly, without guidance – just like the course of a game. The task of sociological research is *to make these blind, uncontrolled processes more accessible to human understanding* by explaining them, and to enable people to orientate themselves within the interwoven social web – which, though created by their own needs and actions, is still opaque to them – and so better to control it. For this to happen, however, the view in which society seems to be centred on oneself or the group with which one identifies has to give way to a view in which oneself or one's own group is no longer the focal point. This transition requires a special effort of detachment just as did the transition from a geocentric to a heliocentric view of the planetary system. The detachment is the difficult part. Even today, this distinction between such sociological detachment and ideological involvement focusing on short-term, present-day problems and values is beyond the grasp of many people, either in thought or action. We often seem to expect to find revelations about the future in the entrails of history, just as the Roman soothsayers did in those of sacrificial animals. Despite all the past and present evidence, it is still hard to come to terms with the idea that though the developmental processes of human society can indeed be explained, they have no pre-existing aim or significance. Their only meaning can be that which people may one day ascribe to sequences of events which now seem random and uncontrollable, once they have learned to understand them and control them better.

Obviously, then, many people will find it confusing that in one way or another the course of social development may take a direction which seems 'meaningful' in terms of their own value system. It will be recalled that Condorcet (1743–94), whom Comte sometimes called his *'vrai père spirituel'*, said during the turmoil of the French revolution that mankind's hopes for the future could be summed up under three headings.[6] These hopes aimed first at an end to inequality between races and countries; secondly at progress towards greater equality between all inhabitants of each country; and thirdly at the perfection of mankind. If the last point is cautiously set aside, it could well be said that mankind has continued to develop since then in the direction Condorcet hoped. But this presents a problem which people often do not fully appreciate. Though there has been a progressive reduction in inequality between and within countries since the end of the eighteenth century, it is absolutely certain that no one consciously planned it or intentionally brought it about. The problem then is this: How can we account for the fact that during this time mechanisms of interweaving, though unplanned and uncontrollable, moved blindly towards increasing humanization of social relationships? First, it is essential to be aware of the blindness of such trends and of the possibility that they might be reversed for unknown reasons. Only then will the sociological problem of analysing and explaining such processes emerge from the shadow cast by what we have called a faith in the pre-established harmony of the ideal and the real.

Nor does this concern only the relatively short-term processes of development which have come about since Condorcet's day. There are many well-known long-term trends in development for which explanation is required. There is the long-term trend towards greater differentiation of all social functions, shown by the proliferation of specialized social activities. There is the tendency for relatively small, single-level attack-and-defence units to become larger and multi-level. There is the long-term civilizing trend towards more even and more thorough control over the emotions, and for people to identify more readily with other people as such, regardless of social origins. There is, within state-societies at least, the trend towards a lessening of inequalities in the distribution of power. But none of these trends takes a straight course, and all are beset with conflicts, often very severe. Social changes in the opposite direction occur too. It is current practice to refer just to 'social change', often without any implication that it may be moving in a consistent direction, whether towards greater or lesser differentiation and complexity. When that implication is there, the concept 'social change' usually applies only to movements towards greater complexity; perhaps it should be applied to change in any consistent direction. At any rate, the real problem is the structure of these changes. Many of these long-term developmental trends can be traced over hundreds or thousands of years. It is beyond human power or foresight to plan and carry out such structured changes. So how are we to interpret the consistency with which human societies develop in a particular direction? How can we explain, for example, the fact that despite all regressions, societies always regain their course leading to greater functional differentiation, multi-level integration and the formation of larger attack-and-defence organizations? Without a framework of developmental theory, the adequate diagnosis and explanation of the sociological problems of contemporary society is scarcely to be expected. Such a framework makes it possible to see how present forms of society have emerged from earlier forms in the way they did. Thus the structural characteristics of nation-states can hardly be clearly distinguished unless a theoretical model is available of how dynastic states develop into nation-states and of the whole process of state formation.[7]

At this point it may be useful to give at least one example of the concepts by means of which different stages of long-term social development can be identified and measured. Among the universal features of society is the *triad of basic controls*. The stage of development attained by a society can be ascertained:

(1)   by the extent of its control-chances over non-human complexes of events – that is, control over what are normally called 'natural events';

(2)   by the extent of its control-chances over interpersonal relationships – that is, over what are usually called 'social relationships';

(3)   by the extent to which each of its members has control over himself as an individual – for, however dependent he may always be on others, he has learned from infancy to control himself to a greater or lesser degree.

These three types of control are interdependent both in their development and in their functioning at any given stage of development. Of the first two types of control, it can be said that control-chances increase gradually as society develops, despite many setbacks. But they do not increase at the same rate. For example, it is highly characteristic of modern societies that their control-chances over non-human natural nexuses are greater and increase faster than their control-chances over interpersonal social nexuses. This difference is reflected in, among other things, the state of development reached by the natural and the social sciences. To a great extent, the latter are still trapped in a characteristic vicious circle like that from which, at an earlier stage of social development, the natural sciences emerged with great difficulty while changing from a magico-mythical to a scientific form. To put it briefly, the less amenable a particular sphere of events is to human control, the more emotional will be people's thinking about it; and the more emotional and fantasy-laden their ideas, the less capable will they be of constructing more accurate models of these nexuses, and thus of gaining greater control over them.

Alternatively, the triad of basic controls could be distinguished in a more familiar way. The first type of control corresponds to what is usually known as technological development. The second type corresponds roughly to the development of social organization; the twin processes of increasing differentiation and increasing integration of social bonds are an example of how this type of control extends. An example of the third type of control is what is known as the 'civilizing process'.[8] The civilizing process is a special case, for unlike the first two types, the direction in which it develops cannot be described simply as an extension or increase of control. In a civilizing process, changes in self-control take place which are not necessarily unilinear. The extension of control over nature is directly interdependent with changes both in self-control and in control over interpersonal relations, as space travel makes spectacularly clear. Even so, it may be useful to warn against the mechanistic idea that the interdependence of the three types of control is to be understood in terms of parallel increases in all three.

6 The problem of the 'inevitability' of social development

When mention is made of such long-term sequences of development as man's increasing control over nature or the progressive division of labour, the question frequently arises whether such developmental processes are 'inevitable'.

To many people it seems self-evident that to describe any long-term trend in the figurational flux of past events is at once to imply a definite prediction for the future. If a long-term civilizing trend has been demonstrated in the patterning of interpersonal behaviour, it is taken for granted that the researcher was trying to prove that people are bound to become more civilized in the future. A model showing how and why a past figuration of relatively uncentralized and undifferentiated social units later developed into a more centralized and complex figuration easily awakens the suspicion that in his research the investigator has projected his aims and wishes for the present and future on to the past. It is assumed that in working out a model of state-formation processes, he ascribed a particular value to the state and wanted to prove that it would always be of particular importance. Anyone concerned with constructing empirically-based models of social development is likely to face repeated obstruction from arguments which have become current largely in opposition to the developmental models of earlier generations.

Generals are sometimes said to plan for a new war as if it were a continuation of the last one. Similarly, there seem to be many received ideas which obstruct the formulation of theories of social development – the same ideas which were used against earlier developmental models. One of them is the notion that diagnosis of a long-term developmental trend in the past necessarily implies that the same trend must continue, automatically and inevitably, into the future. This idea is sometimes made even stronger by the dominant contemporary philosophy of science which, from among all the functions of a scientific theory, selects

as the decisive criterion of scientific validity the function of prediction.

So perhaps it may be useful to discuss the purposes of sociological theories of social development and models of specific
developmental processes – such as the processes of occupational
specialization or of state-formation – based on study of sequences
of past events. Such models are instruments of sociological
diagnosis and explanation. To take one example, nation-states
have usually arisen out of dynastic states, and dynastic states out
of less centralized or tribal organizations. Sometimes the former
arose directly out of the latter, omitting the intermediate stages.
How and why did things happen as they did in each case? Or, to
take another example, out of societies with local markets, little
division of labour, short chains of interdependence and a comparatively humble standard of living, societies came to develop
which had far-reaching trade networks, a great variety of
specialized occupations, long chains of interdependence, and a
comparatively high standard of living. Again, how and why did
the later form of organization develop in every case out of the
earlier? This is the sort of sequence of events for which we are
seeking explanation. A theoretical model of a sequence like this
has a two-fold function – as an explanation and as a scale of
measurement. This is not necessarily a matter of quantitative
measurement, but of plotting differences in figuration. The model
serves to answer such questions as which level in a certain
sequence of development is represented by this or that particular
society, or which stage a society has now reached. A developmental model serves to explain, and thereby to diagnose, but it
also helps to make prognoses. Every explanation makes possible
predictions of one kind or another.

Yet scientific predictions do not by any means have the same
relatively imprecise character as 'prophecies'. For example, it is
not possible to use the theory of evolution as a basis for predictions about the future development of mankind, perhaps into a
race of supermen. It is, however, possible to use the theory of
evolution together with a few other theoretical statements to
predict that no human tooth could ever be found in a seam of
coal – unless it had been put there by a miner! If a human tooth
were ever found in a seam of coal, the whole theory of evolution
would stand in need of substantial correction. Similarly, with the
help of a model of state-formation processes based on the study

of state-formation in the past, certain predictions can be made about the growth processes of contemporary states.

At this point, a simple analogy may help to clarify the functions of theories. In some ways, theories resemble maps. If one stands at point A, where three roads meet, one cannot 'see' directly where these roads lead. One cannot 'see' whether this road or that road leads to a bridge over the river one wants to cross. So one uses a map. To express it differently, a theory gives a man at the foot of a mountain a bird's-eye view of routes and relationships that he cannot see for himself. The discovery of previously unknown relationships is a central task of scientific research. Like maps, theoretical models show the connections between events which are already known. Like maps of unknown regions, they show blank spaces where the connections are not yet known. Like maps, they can be shown by further investigation to be false, and they can be corrected. Perhaps it should be added that, in contrast to maps, sociological models must be visualized in time as well as in space, and thus as four-dimensional models.

It has been said that developmental models can be examined and corrected in the light of further detailed research, and that they can have diagnostic and explanatory as well as predictive functions. This is perhaps best illustrated by a simple reflection, which will also help to clarify what is meant when any social development is said to be 'inevitable'.

A development may be represented schematically as a series of vectors A→B→C→D. Here the letters represent various figurations of people, each figuration flowing from the previous one as the development takes its course from A to D. Retrospective study will often clearly show not only that the figuration at C is a *necessary* precondition for D, and likewise B for C and A for B, but also why this is so. Yet, looking into the future, from whatever point in the figurational flow, we are usually able to establish only that the figuration at B is *one possible* transformation of A, and similarly, C of B and D of C. In other words, in studying the flow of figurations there are two possible perspectives on the connection between one figuration chosen from the continuing flow and another, later, figuration. From the viewpoint of the earlier figuration, the later is – in most if not in all cases – only one of several possibilities for change. From the viewpoint of the later figuration, the earlier one is usually a necessary condition for the formation of the later. It may be useful to add that such sociogenetic connections between earlier and later figurations may be more appropriately expressed if concepts like 'cause' and 'effect' are avoided.

Briefly, the reason for the difference between the two perspectives is this. The degree of pliability and plasticity (or conversely the degree of rigidity) varies widely from one figuration to another. Thus, the range of possibilities for change varies too. One figuration may have much greater potential for change than another. Again, different figurations may have potential for different kinds of change. Then a figuration may have great potential for change without any of the possible changes being developmental in character – none of them involves structural change – change, that is, in the power potential of certain social positions rather than mere changes of personnel among the occupants of those positions. Or a figuration may have little potential for change, yet the chances may be very high that any changes which do occur will be developmental.

In many if not all cases, the figurations formed by interdependent people are so plastic that the figuration at any later stage of the figurational flow is in fact only one of the many possible transformations of an earlier figuration. But as a particular figuration changes into another, a very wide scatter of possible transformations narrows down to a single outcome. In retrospect it is just as feasible to examine the range of potential outcomes as it is to discover the particular constellation of factors responsible for the emergence of this one figuration rather than any other of the possible alternatives.

This explains why a retrospective developmental investigation can often demonstrate with a high degree of certainty *that a figuration had to arise out of a certain earlier figuration or even out of a particular type of sequential series of figurations, but does not assert that the earlier figurations had necessarily to change into the later ones.* So when studying figurational change, it is useful to keep in mind the key idea that every relatively complex, relatively differentiated and highly integrated figuration must be preceded by, and arise out of, relatively less complex, less differentiated and less integrated figurations. Without referring back to the figurational flow which produced them, it would be impossible to understand or explain the interdependence of all the positions in a figuration at a particular time, or the disposition of the people whose socially regulated mutual directedness gives

F

these positions their significance. This statement is not identical with the alternative one with which it is easily confused – that a figurational flow inevitably *had* to produce either *one particular* more complex figuration, or *any* more complex figuration at all. When dealing wih the inevitability of social development, it is essential to distinguish clearly between the proposition that figuration A must inevitably be followed by figuration B, and the proposition that figuration A was a necessary forerunner of figuration B. Connections of the latter kind will be encountered over and over again in investigating problems of social development. And any inquiry into the origins of specific figurations points towards these connections. How have states arisen? What were the origins of capitalism? How do revolutions come about? These and many other similar questions are variations on the theme of whether figuration B was the inevitable result of a preceding figuration A. In this sense, the concept of development refers to a genealogical order. It has to be explained how and why one particular later figuration arose out of another earlier figuration. As long as the existence of the later figuration is simply accepted unquestioningly, and is detached from the figurational flow from which it emerged, it will be possible only to describe, not to understand or explain, how the figuration functions and how the particular positions within it are related to each other.

One source of confusion is that, at present, a scientific 'explanation' is usually understood to be a unilinear causal one. Thus, concepts like capitalism and Protestantism are often used as if they denoted two separate objects existing independently of each other. There are discussions about whether or not Max Weber was right in maintaining that Protestantism was the cause, and capitalism the effect. One of the main differences of developmental sociology is that models are needed to represent figurations in constant flux, with neither beginning nor end. Traditionally, the concept of causality has always implied the search for an absolute beginning – a 'first cause', in fact. So it cannot be expected that the type of explanation needed for research in developmental sociology will be just like explanations which conform to the pattern of traditional models of causality. Instead, changes in figurations are to be explained by other prior changes, and movement by movement, not by a 'first cause' which, so to speak, set everything in motion, and which itself is unmoved.

It is always possible to establish that figuration B had to be preceded by a particular figuration A, although it is not possible to state with equal certainty that figuration A had inevitably to result in figuration B. 'Compelling forces' of this second type are not altogether unknown. Nevertheless, to apply the concept of 'inevitability' to them is to risk becoming entangled in the jungle of physical and metaphysical associations which even today are always evoked whenever 'inevitability' is mentioned in connection with ongoing social development. In this case it might be more accurate and justifiable to talk of varying degrees of possibility and probability, rather than inevitability. To take an obvious example, it can be observed that the figuration of nation-states has at present a very strong tendency to form larger units, which represent a further level of integration and, organizationally, a new tier. Structured tensions and conflicts, which still cannot be controlled to any great extent by those entangled in them, form as always an integral part of this developmental tendency, the dynamics of which are still to be investigated. To give another example, in the last stages of the Roman Empire a strong tendency can be observed towards decentralization and then to disintegration. Although there were repeated counter-movements and efforts at reintegration, it is plain that the tendency gradually gained an impetus which made it irreversible. Another good example is the immanent trend by which a figuration of many units of approximately equal size, competing freely with each other, moves towards a monopolistic figuration. Something of this process is to be seen in the early stages of state-formation, and also in the development of the figuration of competitive economic units within European state-societies in the nineteenth and twentieth centuries. Certainly exogenous factors should not be ruled out when explaining these processes. Nevertheless, the examples given are processes which are to be understood primarily in terms of their own endogenous figurational dynamics. The monopoly mechanism, with which I have dealt in greater detail elsewhere,[1] is a good example of how social forces can be so compelling as to justify the assertion that a particular figuration not yet in existence is very likely to emerge, sooner or later, from an already existing, preceding figuration.

At present, discussion of such problems is often overshadowed by misapprehensions about the application of concepts like 'inevitability' and 'probability'. When applied to the developmental dynamics of figurations, which are composed of people, they do not mean the same as when applied to mechanical causal connections. Perhaps, for many people, relatively undifferentiated conceptual polarities like 'determinacy' and 'indeterminacy' are emotionally satisfying. But they make it difficult to do justice to the many gradations between the two poles which are found in figurations of individuals and their processes of change. Thus, a given figuration within a figurational flow may have a very great (though not unlimited) flexibility, without the later phases of figuration ceasing to be distinctively and recognizably the outcome of certain earlier stages in the figuration. Of course, comparison of two figurations far apart in the same figurational flow, like twelfth- and twentieth-century Britain, reveals relatively little that remains typical of this particular figuration throughout its development. Therefore concepts like culture, civilization and tradition in a static sense may be very misleading when referring to long-term figurational sequences.

On the other hand, by no means all figurations have equally great scope for change. In many cases, the probability is that, if they change at all, it will be in a certain direction. A figurational analysis will often show why this should be so. While such tendencies are not independent of the intentions and actions of the individuals constituting the figuration, nevertheless the form the figuration takes will not be determined by the deliberate plans and intentions of any one of its members, nor by groups of them, nor even by all of them together. For example, in order to explain how relatively highly centralized state-societies have recently developed out of far less centralized and differentiated social units, testable, modifiable models of long-term state-formation processes have to be worked out. However, these are obviously developmental processes of such duration as to be beyond the reach of the contemporary sociological imagination, which is focused on much shorter-term perspectives.

At the present day, it is a reasonably familiar idea that unplanned processes of development in the recent past – such as those of urbanization, industrialization and bureaucratization in the European countries – were quite well-established processes of figurational change with specific structural characteristics of their own. Nonetheless, to speak of the *structure of processes* is still at odds with the static manner in which the concept of structure is often used today. And the structure of certain fundamental transformations of society is seldom seen – including that of the transformation towards increasing centralization, soon followed by increasing control over the central controllers by people hitherto subject to unilateral rule from above.

It is worth remembering that, so far as we know at the moment, state-formation processes have proceeded independently of each other at different times and in different parts of the world. This means that to some degree they must have run their respective courses in accordance with immanent, relatively autonomous figurational dynamics. We are too often satisfied with pseudo-explanations of such parallel figurational changes. They are frequently attributed to the special capacity of certain people, for example the Incas or the Ancient Egyptians, for state-formation. This kind of explanation is makeshift at best. In all these cases, we are clearly dealing with figurations possessing a strong inherent tendency to develop in a given direction. Concepts like probability and inevitability denote observable changes in figuration which cannot – or cannot yet – be controlled and directed by the people who constitute the figuration in question. The modern tendency for contemporary states to become involved in hostile military entanglements is another example of this kind of developmental tendency. The entanglements are created solely by forces exerted by people over people, by groups of men over other groups of men; yet the developmental tendencies are opaque and uncontrollable to the very people whose actions have brought them into being. Such figurations are produced by specific types of interweaving, and it is certainly possible that empirical sociological research may bring us nearer to understanding them. But these developmental trends can be understood, and that understanding communicated to others, only if one is free from total identification with any of the units which together make up the figuration. In other words, insight into the relative autonomy and immanent dynamics of a figuration is impossible for the people who form that figuration as long as they are totally involved and entangled in the altercations and conflicts stemming from their interdependencies. To acquire insight into human figurations, it is necessary to achieve considerable intellectual detachment from the figuration of which one is a member, from its tendencies to change, its 'inevitability', and from the forces which interlocking but opposing groups exert over each other.

Once people have become capable of a large measure of intellectual detachment from the figuration to which they themselves belong, they stand a chance of understanding better the forces which all members exert over each other by reason of their inter-dependence, and the resulting 'inevitability' of figurational change. And if there is a chance of their communicating their insight to the centres of power within the interlocked groups, there will also be an increasing chance of alleviating the pressure of these forces, and ultimately of controlling and directing them. But none of these chances, least of all that of intellectual detachment, depends simply on the personal gifts of individuals in a figuration. Ulti-mately they all depend on the specific characteristics of the figuration itself.

At this point, the vicious circle discussed earlier crops up again. People need to distance themselves from the figuration in which they stand as opponents to each other, if they are to see it as it were from the outside. But they are scarcely in a position to do this sufficiently while the dangers and threats they represent to each other in their interdependence are relatively great, and while they consequently still perceive and think about their mutual entanglement very emotionally. However, the danger and recip-rocal threats can only be diminished if their thinking and behaviour become less affect-laden, which in turn depends on the diminution of the danger. In its relationship to non-human natural forces too, mankind was for a long time just as securely trapped in the vicious circle; the development of men's control over nature represents a feat no less difficult than is escape from the vicious circle of their relationships with each other now. Escape from the earlier trap has by now largely been accom-plished. It would be well worth studying in detail how in that sphere people succeeded in escaping from the vicious circle of self-aggravating 'objective' threats and 'subjective' emotional thought and behaviour – and how long they took to do it.

The social genesis of increasing rationality, bringing in its wake liberation from hitherto uncontrollable forces, represents a long and difficult development. Understanding the specific character of the figurational forces people exert over each other gives a new twist to the old dispute about the problem of determinacy and the 'inevitability' of social development. It makes it possible to steer safely between the Scylla of physics and the Charybdis of meta-physics. Traditional discussions have taken little account of the unique qualities encountered at the level of integration which human society represents. Historically, 'determinism' has usually denoted a mechanical determinacy of the kind observed in causally conditioned physical sequences. In contrast, when the indeterminacy, the 'freedom', of the individual is stressed, it is usually forgotten that there are always simultaneously many mutually dependent individuals, whose interdependence to a greater or lesser extent limits each one's scope for action. In turn, these limitations are an essential part of their humanity. More subtle tools of thought than the usual antithesis of 'determinism' and 'freedom' are needed if such problems are to be solved.

Theory of social development

There are a few remaining points concerning social development which are insufficiently acknowledged in contemporary sociology. The first of them refers to the social unit said to be developing. Nineteenth-century models of development were generally constructed as if one line of development were typical of all mankind and repeated in more or less the same way in every separate society. A separate society was by and large understood to mean the society constituted by a single state.

Nowadays, when we speak of development, we usually have in mind the development of a particular country – either a state-society again, or possibly a tribe. At any rate, present-day attack-and-defence units are implicitly regarded as the units of reference for social development.

It can easily be seen how unsatisfactory it is to limit developmental models to the internal processes of states. One obvious reason for restricting them in this way is that attention is at present concentrated on what could be called the economic aspects of development. But even in the case of the developing countries it is unrealistic to take the onset of processes of so-called economic development as the real nucleus of social development. It is closer to reality to regard processes of differentiation and integration as the hub of the dynamics of social development. Accordingly, the economic aspects of development should be considered along with state-formation processes. The latter are structured aspects of overall development, and certainly in the developing countries it is impossible to separate them from the economic aspects.

But whether examining the development of the countries of the 'Third World' or the continuing development of highly industrialized countries – where processes of state-development play no less a part – the endogenous processes of social development will remain incomprehensible and inexplicable unless the development of the system of states is taken into account at the same time. For each separate state-society is enmeshed in the system of states. There is a tradition that sociologists confine themselves almost entirely to studying processes within societies. Sociological theories, especially in the recent past, have nearly always stuck to a tradition in which the boundaries of states are considered to coincide broadly speaking with those of 'societies'. By general consensus, relationships between states belong to another academic field – that of 'political science'.

The distinction between relationships *within* societies or states and those *between* societies or states is not only wrong in the context of contemporary problems of development – it is always misleading. Whether it is a tribe or a state, the internal development of every attack-and-defence unit is always functionally connected with the development of the prevailing 'balance of power' within the wider figuration in which the several interdependent attack-and-defence units are bound together.

In recent past, the interdependence of intra-society and inter-society developments has become closer and more all-embracing than ever before. Chains of economic interdependence have become tighter and longer. The production of intercontinental weapons, together with other developments of science and technology, have made the internal development of every state-society more significant than ever before for the development of relationships between states – often on a world-wide scale. And *vice versa.* Thus it is even more unrealistic than before to make a theoretical distinction between, on the one hand, a social development seen as internal to the state in question and, on the other hand, the development of relationships between states, of the world-wide balance of power system, or in other words the society of states, which are seen as matters of 'foreign policy'.

This becomes especially apparent if the traditional theoretical treatment of social conflict is compared with the real conflicts acted out before our eyes. Our customary mode of concept formation leads us to make a sharp distinction between two kinds of conflict. Conflicts entailing the use of physical force within a state-society appear conceptually distinct from conflicts involving the use of force between different state-societies, which is the way that the society of states develops. The former are usually classified as revolutions, the latter as wars. The theory of revolutions advanced by Marx and his followers is still to a large extent a vehicle for this conceptual distinction between the structure of violent conflicts on the two levels of integration. From evidence of victorious revolutionary struggles waged by oppressed strata within a single state-society, Marx and Engels deduced that it was theoretically certain that oppressed classes everywhere would some day initiate revolutions. That Marx and Engels did not regard violent conflicts simply as chaotic and unstructured was a great step forward in sociological theory. They viewed them as rooted in the structure of social development, and therefore as possessing structure in their own right. Marx's theory reflected a stage in the development of the social sciences when intra-society developments were regarded as structured and thus as possible objects for scientific research. Yet relationships between states – especially conflicts involving the use of force – were still perceived as unstructured. Therefore conflicts between states were not seen as raw material for the construction of scientific theories. With the increasing interdependence between intra-society and inter-society power struggles – whether in their controlled and non-violent or in their uncontrolled and violent forms – intra-national and international processes of development are interpenetrating and coalescing in many ways.

One example (of the many possible) will be sufficient to demonstrate the impossibility of treating separately developmental processes on the two different levels of integration. Let us look at the dialectics of revolutionary and counter-revolutionary movements on the chessboard of South American republics. As in many other fairly small state-societies, the polarization of larger power groupings on the international scene has led to polarization of the ruling élites within these state-societies. But the strata comprising the mass of the people – the peasants in this case – are squeezed helplessly in a vice. The most powerful state-societies are no less constrained than the smaller, less powerful state-societies which have been drawn into their orbit. Together they form a common figuration – a structural 'clinch'. The balance of power between interdependent states is such that each is so dependent on the others that it sees in every opposing state a threat to its own internal distribution of power, independence and even physical existence. The result of the 'clinch' is that each side constantly tries to improve its power potential and strategic chances in any future warlike encounter. Every increase in the power chances of one side, however slight, will be perceived by the other side as a weakening and a setback in its own position. Within the framework of this figuration it *will* constitute a setback. So countermoves will be set in motion as the weakened side attempts to improve its chances; and these in turn will provoke the first side to make its own countermoves. Mankind's power potentials are thus polarized into two camps – or three if China is included. The members of one group assemble under the banner of communist belief systems of various hues; those of the other group under that of capitalism. One side supports permanent one-party rule; the other side, government by whichever of several parties gains dominance at the time. This polarization has permeated and been superimposed upon local conflicts all over the world.

This is particularly true of all those state-societies situated on the boundaries between the established bastions (or what used to be called the spheres of influence) of the largest attack-and-defence units. The balance of power between these groupings of great powers has become log-jammed, and in many state-societies along the strategic border this has led to splits between zones or sections of the population who lean towards different power blocs. Every time the boundary shifts, it means a disturbance to the flexible balance of tensions between the great power blocs, a potential loss to one side, a potential gain to the other. As long as this figuration of polarized great powers persists, every serious attempt to alter the frontier brings us nearer to the critical phase when armed confrontation between the interdependent opponents slides over into the open use of armed force.

The boundary between the opposing power groups is no longer simply a geographical line, though on the map of Europe and Asia there is still a clear strategic line running from the Pacific Ocean to the Baltic Sea. Apart from that, the growing world-wide interdependence of intra-society and inter-society developments has led to either latent or open confrontations within many medium-sized and small state-societies, between parties supporting one or other of the polarized major societies. It is true that during other phases of human development there have been party divisions within states linked, to a greater or lesser extent, with divisions transcending state boundaries. However, as the web of world-wide relationships grows tighter, these interdependencies spread further and become stronger. Sociologically speaking, war and civil war – and even the threat of them – are interlocking and interpenetrating more and more. The main axis of tension in international relationships exerts a kind of magnetic attraction over many local party divisions within individual state-societies.

A state's internal axis of tension tends to fall into line with the axes of tension between states. In consequence, the strategic boundary between the great powers often runs, either openly or latently, through the middle of individual state-societies. So the less developed, poorer countries are particularly susceptible to outbreaks of armed conflict, and their élites are likely to polarize in line with the all-pervading polarization of the super-powers. All manner of local groups – guerrillas and government troops, revolutionaries and counter-revolutionaries – then conduct petty wars against each other as representatives of the opposing great powers. In highly developed and relatively prosperous societies, the dialectical threat of force does not hinder, and may even positively promote, further development and increasing social wealth; yet in any poor country the polarization of dedicated revolutionaries and counter-revolutionaries usually leads only to further impoverishment. On close examination, aid from the great powers proves to be merely a palliative. Basically it is meant not so much to assist the development of the countries concerned as to gain supporters for one side or the other.

The intermeshing of the two main forms of social violence, those between states ('war') and those within states ('revolution'), is one example among many for which single-level models of social development are no longer adequate. It is equally unsatisfactory to use models of processes of *economic* development as summaries of all that can be said about social development. Theories which treat only the economic aspects of figurational change as structured, can have only a very limited value as guidelines for the empirical investigation or practical solution of problems. Their weakness lies in treating all other aspects, though they are clearly functionally interdependent, as unstructured, as mere accidents, incapable of being scientifically investigated or represented in a theoretical model. Such theories even neglect the state's changing position within the developing society of states. A belief that the overall development of society can be explained or even controlled solely from the economic angle is bound to lead to inaccurate judgements and misguided plans. What are needed instead are two-level sociological models of development, which include processes of integration as well as differentiation, international as well as internal developments, and recognize all of them as structured aspects of the overall process.

People often seem deliberately to forget that social developments have to do with changes in human interdependence and with changes in men themselves. But if no consideration is given to what happens to people in the course of social change – changes in figurations composed of people – then any scientific effort might as well be spared. Whatever else it may mean, social development always means changes in the nature and relationship of social positions, occupied by various groups of people. It must always and unavoidably mean that in the course of development certain social positions or groups of positions surrender, in whole or in part, their functions within a functional complex. At the same time, other groups of positions (sometimes older, more often quite new ones) gain new functions and acquire importance within the wider society. So it is inadequate, in analysing social change let alone in planning it, to confine oneself to intellectual manipulation of seemingly impersonal concepts like capital investment, wages, productivity and so on.

It will not do to pay most attention to the new, which is just emerging, while neglecting the old, which is declining or disappearing in the course of development. New positions with new functions may arise; the functions of older positions may be either augmented or reduced, maybe to nothing. But it is wrong to think that two currents within a figuration, one in the ascendant, the other declining in the course of social development, can be regarded as impersonal happenings on an extra-human plane. In real terms, this rise and fall means the rise and fall of groups of people. It means that certain groups will have greater power chances; it means that others, losing some or all of their functions, will forfeit all or part of their power chances.[2]

One of the most astonishing features of many sociological and economic theories is that they scarcely acknowledge the central part played in every social development by tensions and conflicts. The impression is often given that social scientists imagine semiconsciously that they will unintentionally bring about such tensions and conflicts if they include them in their models of society.

Or they are afraid of seeming to approve of these tensions and conflicts. *But social tensions and conflicts will never be banished from society by suppressing them in theories.* It is easy to see that tensions and conflicts between groups which are losing functions and those acquiring new or increased functions, are a vital structural feature of all development. In other words, it is not just a question of personal, mainly accidental tensions and conflicts, though the people involved usually see them as such. From the viewpoint of the intermeshing groups, they can sometimes be seen as expressions of personal animosity, sometimes as consequences of the ideology of one side or the other. On the contrary, however, this is a matter of *structured* conflicts and tensions. In many cases they and their results form the very kernel of a process of development.

Systematic sociological studies of these displacements of function and consequent shifts in power balances at the centre of developmental processes are still in short supply. However, what was said above about the structural properties of social developments can be illustrated by one salient example. Though familiar, its significance is easily overlooked. In the course of certain developmental processes in European societies during the nineteenth and twentieth centuries, there was a sometimes gradual, sometimes rapid erosion of the functions of the positions of princes and noblemen. Until the eighteenth century, in all the larger states, subversion and revolts always aimed to overthrow one sovereign in favour of another, or to increase or reduce the power of sections of the nobility in relation to the sovereign, or in relation to other strata of the nobility. But these efforts were never permanent and seldom did they aim to abolish the positions of sovereigns and nobles as such. Even after the execution of the king of England (Charles I, in 1649), the position of the revolutionary leader (Cromwell) soon reverted to a monarchic position when the returning representative of the old royal dynasty (Charles II, reigning 1660-85) reassumed the traditional position of king. Closer analysis might easily reveal the structural properties of pre-industrial state-societies responsible for the eventual outcome of such revolts. For despite all their vagaries, these societies always reverted to a figuration which made small privileged strata into nobles and monarchs, and vested this kind of élite with great power chances, in comparison with those of the bulk of the population. Since then, power has been gradually draining away from the positions of nobility in all European societies alike; in many cases these positions have vanished altogether. Yet non-sociological accounts of the development of European society often give the impression that this was all a chance occurrence, some unique historical event.

Nonetheless, closer study of the course of the French Revolution shows plainly that even before the Revolution, beneath the surface of the *ancien régime,* the positions of king and nobility had been suffering from loss of function as society in pre-industrial France became more commercialized. The privileges associated with their positions, in particular the unequal distribution of taxes in their favour, seemed to many contemporary observers to bear no relation to their 'function for the nation', as the Abbé Sieyès put it. If the course taken by this development is examined in detail, it is apparent that the revolutionary expropriation of the functions of the king and nobility was not brought about simply by the onslaught of the rebelling strata. It was also initiated by the understandable incapacity of the king and nobles to adapt themselves to the fact that their positions were gradually losing functions, and by their refusal to agree to a reduction in their privileges corresponding to their declining power potential.

The rise and fall of groups within figurations, and the concomitant structural tensions and conflicts, are central to all developmental processes. They have to be placed at the centre of any sociological theory of development. Otherwise it is impossible to come to grips with the central theoretical and practical problem with which sociologists are confronted again and again. That problem is whether and to what extent uncontrolled conflicts and tensions between different groups of people can be brought under the conscious control and direction of those involved in them, or whether such tensions and conflicts can only be resolved through violence, either as revolutions within or as wars between states.

Notes and references

Introduction

1. For simplicity's sake only the most elementary types of people's needs for each other, and of their corresponding bonds with each other, are shown in this diagram – only their affective valencies (see page 134ff). There are many other types which have similar functions. People need each other, are directed towards and bonded to each other as a result of the division of labour, of occupational specialization, of integration into tribes or states, of a common sense of identity, and of their shared antagonism for others or their hatred and enmity towards each other.

The main task of Figure 2 is to facilitate the reorientation of sociological models and concepts, which becomes possible if one stops viewing human beings, including oneself, as completely autonomous units and perceives them instead as semi-autonomous units needing each other, dependent on and bonded to each other in a great variety of ways. The diagram indicates that unstable power balances (see page 74) and related trials of strength are among the basic properties of all human relationships, whether they are relatively simple relationships between two people as in marriage, or multi-member figurations such as towns or states, formed by great numbers of people.

2. See N. Elias, 'Problems of Involvement and Detachment', *British Journal of Sociology*, vol. 7, no. 3, 1956, pp. 226-52.

1 Sociology – the questions asked by Comte

1. Many men of the period used the word 'positive' in this sense. Comte, like Turgot before him, used it as an antonym for all that they regarded as speculative, whether it took the form of theology or philosophy. Comte called his theory of sciences 'positive philosophy' in order to distinguish it as a scientific philosophy (or, as we might say, a scientific theory) of science, as opposed to the speculative philosophical theories of science current in his time as in ours.

2. Auguste Comte, *Cours de philosophie positive*, 1830-42, 5th ed., Paris, 1907, vol. 1, p. 5. (This and other excerpts have been freshly translated from the French.)

3. *Ibid*. p. 2.

4. *Ibid*. p. 5.

5. *Ibid*. p. 6.

6. *Ibid*. p. 52.

7. Wolfgang Wiener, *Organismen, Strukturen, Maschinen: Zu eine Lehrer vom Organismus*, Frankfurt am Main, 1959, pp. 64, 68.

8. Comte, pp. 15-16 (my italics).

3   Game models

1. See N. Elias, 'Problems of involvement and detachment', *British Journal of Sociology*, vol. 7, no. 3, 1956, pp. 226-52.

2. What we call 'figuration' with reference to the constituent parts is identical with what we call 'structure' with reference to the composite unit. If we speak of the structure of societies and of the figuration or pattern of bonding of the individuals who form these societies, we are in fact speaking of the same thing as seen from different angles.

3. E. E. Evans-Pritchard's well-known analysis of the function of feuds between Nuer lineage groups is an instructive example of the teleological use of the concept of function. It is debased into a concept of the purpose served in conserving an existing social system. 'The function of the feud, viewed in this way, is therefore to maintain the structural equilibrium between opposed tribal segments which are, nevertheless, politically fused in relation to larger units.' (E. E. Evans-Pritchard, *The Nuer*, Oxford, 1940, ch. 3, p. 159.) It might be more appropriate to say that during the period of the inquiry the functions which the segmentary groups possessed for each other as allies and fellow-tribesmen outweighed their function as rivals to each other.

4. A detailed examination of functions and power in relations between specialized groups is to be found in N. Elias, *Die Höfische Gesellschaft*, Neuwied and Berlin, 1970, ch. II and IV.

5. There is no need to emphasize the critical reflection on action and interaction theories, which pay little if any attention to the structure of pressures which one person's or one group's 'action' exercises upon that of others.

6. The concept of 'impaired fuctioning' in the context of observable social processes is not to be confused with Merton's concept of 'dysfunction', which is useless for sociological research. The Mertonian concept is based on a predetermined set of values; it refers to an ideal image of harmoniously functioning static societies – an image which does not correspond to anything observable in real life.

7. Many societies which have not yet developed into states nevertheless operate on more than two levels. Even in a federation of tribes as simply and loosely integrated as that of the old Iroquois, the federal procedure when an individual wanted to put a proposal to the federation was as follows (the source is a contemporary account by the Rev. Asher Wright, quoted in Edmund Wilson, *Apologies to the Iroquois,* London, 1960, p. 1974):

A measure must first gain the assent of the proposer's family, then his clan, next of the four related clans in his end of the council house, then of his nation, and then in due course of order the business would be brought up before the representatives of the Confederacy. In the reverse order the measures of the general council were sent down to the people for their approval. It was a standing rule that all action should be unanimous. Hence the discussions, without any known exception, were always continued till all opposition was reasoned down, or the proposed measure abandoned.

8. H. J. Königsberger, '*Dominium regale* or *dominium et regale?:* Monarchies and Parliaments in Early Modern Europe', in *Human Figurations: Essays for Norbert Elias,* ed. P. Gleichmann, J. Goudsblom and H. Korte, Amsterdam, 1977.

9. N. Elias and J. Scotson, *The Established and the Outsiders,* London, 1965.

10. My colleague Richard Brown of the University of Durham, who was kind enough to read this part of the manuscript, drew it to my attention that calculations of this kind have already appeared in E. F. C. Brech, *Organisation,* London and New York, 1957, p. 77 *et seq.,* even though in the context of rather different theoretical problems.

4 Universal features of human society

1. Space here is too limited for me to give enough examples to prove how much confusion still reigns in this field. But it ought

to be mentioned that even a scholar of the stature of Konrad Lorenz, both a theoretical and an empirical leader in his field, can forget the simple distinction between human modes of behaviour which are largely learned, and the modes of behaviour of non-human organisms, which are to a large extent automatic and not learned. He observes superficial parallels between certain modes of human social behaviour in accordance with norms and the social behaviour of greylag geese and wolves. On his own ground, animal sociology, Lorenz habitually relies on careful, minutely observed work as a basis for theory formation. For this very reason one might have expected him to familiarize himself with the results of sociological research on human societies, and to pay the same careful and minute attention to detail before drawing conclusions about human aggression and its regulation from his knowledge of aggression and its regulation in animal societies. (See Konrad Lorenz, *On Aggression,* trans. Marjorie Laske, Methuen, London, 1967.) It can easily be shown that the generation of norms, and the whole social imprinting of human aggressive behaviour in the course of people's relationships with each other, are extraordinarily variable. They may vary greatly from one society to another, or even between different strata of the same society. They differ greatly between industrial societies and societies where the ruling strata are composed of warriors. Material relevant to this problem is to be found in Norbert Elias, *Über den Prozess der Zivilisation,* 2nd ed., Berne and Munich, 1969. (An English translation, *The Civilising Process,* is to be published shortly.)

The only way to establish with any certainty whether and to what extent the root of all aggressive behaviour lies in a behavioural tendency common to the whole species is to carry out thorough comparative studies in many societies at varying stages of social development. As already stated, human behaviour as we observe it is always the outcome of an often very complex balance of tensions between cortical and sub-cortical impulses. Lorenz seems to neglect to take into account the internalization of learned behavioural controls which is possible in human nature but not, if his researches are to be trusted, in the nature of the greylag goose. It is out of the question to believe that the natural history of aggression runs in a straight line directly from the stickleback to man.

While on this subject, it might be useful to point out another misapprehension which lies at the root of the theses of the philosopher Arnold Gehlen. He seems to confuse the greater plasticity of human instinctive behaviour, which implies a greater ability on the part of man to control the instincts, with mankind as a species possessing weak instincts. The available evidence hardly justifies the conclusion that because human instincts are the most malleable and the most amenable to control, they must necessarily be weak. There is no proof at all that human instincts are any weaker than those of lions, apes or sparrows.

2. B. L. Whorf, *Language, Thought and Reality: Selected Writings*, MIT, Press, Cambridge, Mass., 1956. Reading Whorf is a great pleasure, because with a wide knowledge of the field he vigorously attacks problems which are urgently in need of investigation. The systematic comparison of types of languages earlier undertaken by Humboldt seems likely to be fruitful for sociology. Whorf, however, began with the assumption which Lévi-Strauss later elaborated, that the structure of language is an independent stratum of reality existing in and for itself. We may well forgive linguists if now and again they lose sight of the fact that what we reify as language is no more than a system of signals which people use to communicate with each other. It is not so easy to understand what Lévi-Strauss has in mind when he takes the structure of a language as a model, even as a matrix of social structure, instead of simply relating the structure of a language to the structure of the society in which it is spoken. (See Claude Lévi-Strauss, *Structural Anthropology*, trans. Claire Jacobson and Brooke Grundfest Schoepf, Basic Books, New York, 1963.) Whorf himself did not quite succeed in avoiding the pitfall of treating a spoken language as something unevolved and unchangeable. He thus tended to neutralize the threat which a radical critique must pose not only to particular concepts but to the whole mode of concept formation traditional in a society – to the forms of language and thought which are taken for granted. A critique of this kind threatens the confidence of such a society. To suggest that the habitual forms of thought – the indispensable aids for sifting experience, and the normal instruments of orientation – are only valid within the framework of one's own society, is to place oneself and others at risk of succumbing to relativistic despair.

However, this danger can only persist while radical criticism of forms of speech and thought is not combined with attempts to relax them sufficiently for people to become aware of their inadequacy in regard to the tasks for which they are used. In short, the risk can be averted by using such a critique to open up possibilities of making a society's customary modes of speaking and thinking more suitable to their tasks, if that is necessary. Among linguists, there are some structuralists who sometimes refer to the structure of languages as if the existing structure of a society's language were a concomitant of that society, naturally belonging to it for all eternity. This is merely another version of the idea that the present condition of a particular society – and of its language too in this case – is fixed and unchangeable.

3. A brief sociological study of this swing of the pendulum is to be found in the Preface to Norbert Elias, *Über den Prozess der Zivilisation*, 2nd ed., Berne and Munich, 1969.

4. Emile Durkheim, *The Division of Labour in Society*, trans. G. E. Simpson, Macmillan, New York, 1933, p. 350.

5. Cf. Norbert Elias, *Über den Prozess der Zivilisation*, and Elias, *Die Höfische Gesellschaft*, Neuwied and Berlin, 1970.

6. Emile Durkheim, *The Rules of Sociological Method*, Free Press, New York, 1964, p. 28.

7. See R. Brown and A. Gilman, 'The Pronouns of Power and Solidarity', in P. P. Giglioli (Ed.), *Language and Social Context*, Penguin, Harmondsworth, 1972.

8. See Figure 2, page 15 and note 1 to the Introduction on page 175.

9. These problems are dealt with in greater detail in Norbert Elias and Eric Dunning, 'Dynamics of sport groups with special reference to football', *British Journal of Sociology*, vol. 17, no. 4, 1966, pp. 388-401.

5 Human interdependencies – problems of social bonds

1. Talcott Parsons, 'Psychology and sociology', in John Gillin (Ed.), *For a Science of Social Man*, New York, 1954, p. 84. Here Parsons establishes that 'the structure of the personality is a kind of "mirror-image" of the structure of the social object-system', and then, as a kind of warning, immediately adds that 'We should be very careful in the interpretation of these statements. They clearly do not mean that a personality as a system is simply a reflection of the social situation at the time. This would be a negation of the postulate of the independence of the personality system.' He makes no attempt to explain how the idea of personality as a mirror-image of society is to be harmonized with his

postulating the independence of the individual. The two assertions simply stand side by side in Parsons's system of arguments, never really reconciled.

2. This constellation of problems is dealt with in more detail in Norbert Elias, 'Sociology and Psychiatry', in S. H. Foulkes and G. S. Prince (Eds.), *Psychiatry in a Changing Society,* London, 1969, pp. 117-44.

3. This problem will remain until all former attack-and-defence units have been effectively integrated into one – mankind.

4. See Elias, *Über den Prozess der Zivilisation,* 2nd ed., Berne and Munich, 1969.

5. Allen M. Sievers, *Revolution, Evolution and the Economic Order,* Englewood Cliffs, N.J., 1962, p. 1.

6. Cf. S. Krynska, *Entwicklung und Forstschritt nach Condorcet und Comte,* Berne, 1908, p. 27.

7. A model of state-formation processes – though of course it could be extended and improved upon – is to be found in Elias, *Über den Prozess der Zivilisation.*

8. *Ibid.,* vol. I.

6 The problem of the 'inevitability' of social development

1. See N. Elias, *Über den Prozess der Zivilisation,* 2nd ed., Berne and Munich, 1969.

2. One of Marx's greatest achievements, and the most helpful to the development of sociology, was that he recognized the problem of the rise and fall of social classes to be central to a theory of social development, and attempted to investigate it empirically. However, like other early theorizing, his model was permeated with the metaphysics of his values. He was unable to free himself from the idea that strata which were rising were 'good', and those which were falling were 'bad'. He traced very sharply the battlefront of the rising industrial middle classes against the lower industrial working classes which were also in the ascendant. On the other hand, he neglected the struggle (still very evident at that time) of the rising middle classes to catch up with the traditional aristocratic–military–landowning ruling classes, almost as if the French Revolution had in fact destroyed the latter's power altogether. From his vantage point in the battle, he was unable to see sufficiently clearly that within both the industrial bourgeoisie and the industrial working class there were

strata rising and falling, as indeed there always are. In his day perhaps it was hardly possible to grasp that. We are now in a position to construct a much more comprehensive and differentiated model of the rise and fall of social strata. But in sociology, as in other sciences, every later theory develops both as a continuation of earlier theories and yet as a critical departure from them.

Index